HOMOSEXUALITY IN AFRICA

Bart Luirink and Madeleine Maurick

HOMOSEXUALITY IN AFRICA

A disturbing love

Uitgeverij Aspekt

HOMOSEXUALITY IN AFRICA

© 2016 Uitgeverij ASPEKT
© Bart Luirink and Madeleine Maurick

Amersfoortsestraat 27, 3769 AD Soesterberg, Netherlands
info@uitgeverijaspekt.nl
www.uitgeverijaspekt.nl

Translation from Dutch: Christopher Chambers
Proof reading: Devi Pillay
Cover design: Maarten Bakker
Cover picture: © Zanele Muholi. Courtesy of Stevenson, Cape Town, Johannesburg
Inside: Aspekt Graphics

ISBN: 9789461539434
NUR: 600

Dutch version ISBN: 9789461538130

All rights reserved. No reproduction copy or transmission of this publication may be made without written permission.

Contents

Foreword   7

Chapter 1: *The 'twin banana'*   11
The long road to equal rights in South Africa.
A brief history.

Chapter 2: *Stoking the fire*   60
Hot on the heels of South Africa's monumental changes, the Zimbabwean President Robert Mugabe comes out of the closet as the commander-in-chief of Africa's anti-gay brigade. The ensuing witch-hunt is locking horns with the forces of change.

Chapter 3: *You say yes, I say no*   81
A ritual dance to the same tune. With an unwillingness to compromise and little enthusiasm to see the opposing view, the warring parties are each claiming the upper hand by using 'facts', anthropological discoveries, interpretations of religious texts, and assumptions based on characteristics of 'the' African culture.

Chapter 4: *Is Africa different or just the same?*   94
Men are women and footballers aren't. Fantasies run wild regarding an assumed African sexuality. But is Africa really so different?

Chapter 5: *An obsession extraordinaire*   113
The battle for the heart of the Anglican Church. African bishops are feeling short-changed. Exclusive: an interview with the former Archbishop Desmond Tutu.

Chapter 6: *All welcome: porn in the church!*   **129**
The alliance between evangelicals, politicians and the Ugandan first lady. Now that Christian fundamentalists are losing ground in the United States, a cultural war against homosexuals has been relocated to the 'dark continent'. Do Africans really believe everything that white evangelicals tell them? A look behind the scenes in Uganda.

Chapter 7: *"Sodo-Miites"*   **169**
A glimmer of pink light is coming into view on Africa's horizon. Which of Africa's (former) rulers are speaking out for tolerance and equal rights? Contemporary African literature is a half-closed book for homosexuals. Also: the 'pink soaps' coming out of Nollywood, and the international breakthrough of gay and lesbian photographers and artists.

Chapter 8: *Relationship issues*   **195**
Their struggle, our struggle. Subsidies and solidarity. At the end of the nineties the gay English-Nigerian footballer Justin Fashanu took his own life in a lock-up garage in London. To Fashanu, Britain had nothing to offer. These days, British politicians are quick to condemn homophobia anywhere in the world. An account of a trying relationship burdened with a history of colonial oppression and domination. Also: the role of donors, diplomats and do-gooders.

Foreword

Drought, ebola, war and plagues of locusts. It's hard to imagine, but many of the disasters that afflict Africa are being laid at the door of gays and lesbians. Sexual minorities are, in the words of the *'anti's'*, 'worse than dogs and pigs'. So, it's open season and in many African countries tough anti-gay legislation is becoming even more draconian. Homosexual women and men are the victims of hate campaigns, assault and rape. Advocates of equal rights are accused of subverting African traditions and culture. Opponents claim the intention is to destroy the very fabric that binds communities and families; accusations that help give credence to the idea that supporters of equal rights (with a guiding hand of the West) are deliberately undermining the foundations of the postcolonial framework. The rise of LGBT (*lesbian, gays, bisexuals & transgenders*) movements in Africa is evidence of the comprehensive changes taking place there. Criticism being voiced by gay activists over out-dated and intransigent power structures isn't just an expression of disobedience emenating from a small minority - it's a call for change that will ultimately affect all Africans.

In 1996, the right to be free from discrimination on the grounds of sexual orientation was written into South Africa's constitution. After the apartheid era, Nelson Mandela's vision was that *all* South Africans should be free and equal. The scope of the constitutional clause was a first for the continent and indeed for the world; and was followed ten years later with the legislation of same-sex marriage. Encouraged by these changes homosexuals across Africa are beginning to climb out of the closet, and in a salute to the international trend, are proudly calling themselves 'gay' and 'lesbian', forming interest groups and taking to the street. The accusation that homosexuality is something alien and 'western' is being contemptuously pushed aside. And in this struggle for equality they are also keenly aware of its strong associations with the fight for democracy, against the abuse of power and a desire for personal freedom in Africa.

So there is considerably more at stake than just the right to do what you want in the bedroom. Gay communities in Africa are shaking up the old order and challenging the omnipotence of potentates and patriarchs, orthodox church leaders and frustrated youths. Their actions relate not just to sexual freedom but are also challenging the social control enjoyed by the entrenched community leaders, the servants of the one party system and the preachers of an inflexible and intolerant faith. No wonder that so much venom and violence has been levelled at this fledging African liberation movement.

In the past few years we have visited more than ten countries on the continent in an attempt to find answers to the question of how one can more fully understand the African LGBT movement and the sometimes ruthless fight against it. We spoke to those both for and against, the participants in the conflict, observers and analysts. It has produced a contrasting image of both disillusionment and hope. It has also made us treat frequently heard platitudes with a degree of caution. One would be forgiven for believing that genocide is currently in full swing against sexual minorities, that gay life is non-existent, and that the continent's entire population is vehemently anti-gay. It's been all too easy to dismiss Africa as a lost cause - a pitiful and frightening monolith. What we observed, in the English speaking regions of Africa, is considerably more complex. What is equally striking are the links that exist between the struggle of a small minority for equal rights, the hunting down of warlords and the relentless pursuit of raw materials. A book has now grown out of our observations and talks with activists, lawyers, church leaders, politicians, writers and scientists - a book that charts the complex history of Africa's youngest liberation movement.

Bart Luirink
Madeleine Maurick

Chapter 1

The 'twin banana'

With a constitution that guarantees the right to be free from discrimination on the grounds of sexual orientation, along with the official recognition of same-sex marriage, South Africa has been at the vanguard of a continent-wide struggle for freedom. During the transitional period from apartheid to democracy, the country's gay rights movement seized the opportunity to guarantee that the newly acquired freedoms would be for everyone. A brief history.

In the autumn of 2011, the South African President Jacob Zuma announces that his nomination for Chief Justice, the head of the Constitutional Court, will be judge Mogoeng Mogoeng. It leads to a storm of criticism. According to numerous commentaries, there's now a chance that a deeply religious, uber-conservative man will become the most important judge in the country. Will this be the person responsible for safeguarding a fledgling constitution that is only fifteen years old, and guarantees equal rights for women and the right to an abortion? Furthermore, a constitution that explicitly declares the right to be free from discrimination on the grounds of sexual orientation, and one modified around the time of Nelson Mandela's release in 1990 to incorporate a moratorium on the death penalty - a constitution passed, almost unanimously, into law in 1996 and lauded as perhaps the most comprehensive and progressive in the world.

South Africa, therefore, has a reputation to uphold, especially when it comes to human rights. Could this be entrusted to someone who is a leading member of Winners Chapel International, a 'happy-clappy' church with a million followers led by the billionaire Nigerian bishop David Oyedepo? After Zuma's announcement, media reports suggest that Mogoeng might personally have treated homosexual members of the congregation for their 'abnormality' and is convinced a cure for homosexuality is possible. There are also suggestions he is sympathetic to calls for the re-instatement of the death sentence and that he finds abortion abhorrent. A number of his previous decisions as a judge hint that he considers rape within marriage as *not* rape. He had also been particularly lenient in cases involving the physical abuse of women. In one decision in the court of appeal, he overruled a two-year jail sentence in favour of a fine for a man who had tied his wife to the bumper of his car and then driven her at fifty kilometres an hour over a gravelled road. Mogoeng had found the punishment too harsh declaring the incident had been instigated "due to provocation by the complainant". Sentences handed down for rape were reduced or even overturned by Mogoeng because "the parties involved were known to each other". He also imposed the minimum sentence possible on a man who had raped a seven-year old girl, reasoning that the "injuries were not serious".

Mogoeng's more recent voting behaviour, since his promotion to the Constitutional Court in 2009, also gave South African progressives cause for concern. He is the sole voice against the decision of the Court to regard the word 'gay' as *not* being a term of abuse. The case arose after a complaint from a teacher whose pupils had photo-shopped his head to the naked torso of a man. The inference was that the teacher was gay. The Court decrees there is no question that it was intended as offensive. The 'victim' was being accused of belonging to a group that was, according to the constitution, as equal as any other group in society. So why would it be an insult to be called gay? To emphasise this further, the Court expands on its verdict by adding that this also includes lesbians, women, black people, the aged, men, atheists, Muslims, Zulus, Christians and Afrikaners. Mogoeng gives no explanation for his differing opinion.

A few months before Zuma makes his intention clear, the South African law professor Pierre de Vos postulates on the choice the president is likely to make and what that decision could mean. Will he appoint a conservative man who is likely to impede the Court's ability to carry forward progressive laws, or will he choose a more enlightened man or woman who, within the existing framework of the law, will build on its modern principles, such as rights for women and LGBTs (Lesbian, Gay, Bisexual and Transgender), a ban on the death penalty and so on? In its short life, the Constitutional Court has shown that the more progressive clauses of the constitution are not just meaningless additions. In countless decisions, the country's highest judges have reconfirmed the equal status of women. It also intervened during the debacle surrounding the AIDS policy of the former President Thabo Mbeki and his health minister Tshabalala-Msimang. Both were accused of dragging their feet in implementing a coherent and effective health programme to counteract the devastating consequences of the disease. Tshabalala-Msimang had been openly promoting the benefits of garlic and beetroot as remedies. The Court also stretched its mandate to the limit with its declarations relating to the somewhat vague constitutional wording of issues such as the right to housing, education, land ownership and health care. When the South African parliament appeared to be delaying legislation to legalise gay marriage, the Court forced it to introduce such measures within a year.

President Zuma overlooks those candidates who fit De Vos' progressive profile and instead recommends Mogoeng – an unequivocal traditionalist and a man after his own heart. In the run-up to his election as president, Zuma made no secret of his polygamous beliefs, marrying a number of times to considerably younger women, following the payment of *lobola* – a dowry. In his defence against an accusation of rape in 1996, he proclaims that the woman in question had goaded him into having sex by wearing provocative clothing. According to Zuma, "in the Zulu culture, you cannot just leave a woman if she is ready". When asked his views on homosexuality during the presidential election campaign in 2009, he recollects a memory from his childhood: "When I was growing up, *ungqingili* (homosexual) could not stand in front of me, I would knock him out." About a year after this episode, Zuma appoints the former journalist Jon Quelane as ambassador to Uganda; a self-declared homophobe would be representing South Africa in a country where the persecution of homosexuals was the order of the day. (In 2011, Quelane was found guilty of 'hate-speech' by South Africa's Equality Court and was subsequently removed from his post in Kampala).

On Saturday 3 September 2011, Mogoeng appears before the Judicial Service Commission (JSC), a special body set up to screen candidates for their suitability for high legal posts. The session is being screened live on South African television. The public gallery is crammed full of people from defenders representing women, gays, human rights organisations and the media. A visibly nervous Mogoeng must endure endless questioning over the more notable decisions of his legal career. After reading out approximately forty pages, in which he defends himself against accusations in the media, he confirms that he did indeed see his forthcoming appointment as a sign of God's will. He reasons that this is not inconsistent with the principle of the division of church and state enshrined in the constitution. He adds that he attaches great importance to the non-sexist, gay friendly clauses contained therein. The atmosphere then becomes highly charged. Dikgang Moseneke, the Deputy Chief Justice considered by many to be a more suitable candidate for the top job, questions Mogoeng over his singular decision concerning the 'terms of abuse' case. The judge declares that he had had insufficient time to go into the matter, but now considers his decision to be "misguided" and "in hindsight, mistaken". He regrets this and offers his excuses. In reaction to Moseneke's remark that it is perhaps a little on the late side, Mogoeng snaps back: "There's no need to be sarcastic, sir!" The candidate then goes further by declaring that, at the time, he ought to have given more reasons for having voted out of step with the other judges. "So that there is no confusion, I would like to state that I am not opposed to homosexuals and lesbians asserting their constitutional right to be treated equally."

The exchanges between the two judges dominate the coverage in most newspapers and radio and television reports. Some conclude that Mogoeng's climb down is a victory for the LGBT movement, and a sign of progress – after all, Moseneke was re-affirming their rights, and so defending equal rights would no longer be left exclusively to those specifically championing sexual minorities. The second most important judge in the country was now clearly declaring his support, in a similar fashion to the way a number of heterosexual African National Congress (ANC) politicians had done in the past.

For many though, Mogoeng's *mea culpa* rings hollow. They suspect the judge of saying what he thinks the panel wants to hear, so as not to jeopardize his chances. Just before the hearing, he had announced to members of his church in Soweto that he would shortly become one of the most important men in the country. Mogoeng was burning with ambition.

The day after the hearing, the JSC makes its decision known. With 16 votes for, and 7 against, the commission concludes that Mogoeng is fit to take up the position that Zuma has so pointedly nominated him for.

Gay rights activists suspect the new Chief Justice is a wolf in sheep's clothing. On the day the appointment is announced, and with a clear feeling for understatement, a spokesperson for the country's LGBT movement declares "one cannot be reassured that the defence of rights that have existed for only twenty years are in safe hands."

*

The history of the South African gay rights movement begins behind prison walls. In fact, a strong case can be made that the very start of gay activism in the whole of Africa begins with the heated discussions taking place between South Africa's political prisoners in the middle of the 1980s. Groups did exist from the 1970s onwards in South Africa and Zimbabwe (then known as Rhodesia – named after the British homosexual imperialist Cecil Rhodes), but these are more like social networks whose members are predominantly white and largely silent over the racist policies of the governing parties. They feel more European than African. At best, one could say they're afraid to draw attention to themselves with what will be viewed as anti-apartheid actions. However, a considerable number sympathize openly with the politics of segregation and white superiority. For them, it seems of little consequence that the laws of both countries still contain anti-gay clauses, a legacy of the Rhodes era.

A lesbian group exists in the Egyptian capital Cairo from as early as the 1970s, but the members of this underground social network consider themselves to be more a part of the Arab world than of Africa.

Back to the prison. It is the spring of 1985. South African police have arrested twenty-two activists accused of the murder of a policeman. Among those arrested are Mosiuoa Lekota, Frank Chikane and Popo Molefe, three of the leaders of the United Democratic Front (UDF) a coalition of hundreds of community based organisations that supports the still banned ANC. Simon Nkoli is also detained – a student leader from Sebokeng, a township not far from Johannesburg. Not long before his imprisonment, he has come out within his organisation as gay. The announcement leads to the usual discussion over rights and wrongs, but Nkoli is subsequently chosen as the regional chair of the student movement. "You have to take me as I am," he explains to his fellow activists. And they do – not the slightest reference to his sexuality is made thereafter.

Nkoli's cellmates know nothing of his sexual preference. To them, he is just a comrade and a brother-in-arms. His private life is not an issue. It's just assumed that he's heterosexual. But then something happens within the prison that forces the student leader to nail his colours to the mast. A fierce discussion breaks out over the behaviour of one of their colleagues who is believed to have had sex with one of the guards. The incident angers Lekota and the other leaders of the group. At first, they are enraged that one of their own has allowed something to happen between himself and an accessory to the enemy. They demand to know whether it was just a short dalliance or something of a more serious nature. Has he given the guard any incriminating information? They're worried that their accusers will use the incident to taint the whole group and brand them all as *moffies* (queers). However, during the course of the discussion, they begin to take a more strident course by declaring that homosexuality is 'anti-social behaviour'. The 'democratic movement' must remain free from such stigmas; the values of a democratic South Africa are not compatible with a sexual orientation considered immoral. Lekota then declares the matter closed once the offending colleague has offered his apologies and has sworn that it would not happen again. It's the moment for a shy Nkoli to announce in a soft voice: "But what about me?"

The discussion starts afresh. At first within the group itself, and then spreading to other cells and sections of the prison. Nkoli stands his ground against a barrage of prejudice and accusations. After his release, he declares he is determined to help establish a non-racial LGBT movement open to everyone. The antipathy shown by his comrades emboldens him further and he ensures the subject is not swept under the carpet. When Nkoli is threatened with ejection from the group, the lawyer George Bizos steps into the fray. He offers to help Nkoli and makes it clear to Lekota that he will cease defending them as a whole if one is thrown out. Bizos was born in Greece and speaks with the authority of a man who helped defend Nelson Mandela and his compatriots during the Rivonia trial in the 1960s. Nkoli's accusers are begrudgingly forced to back down.

In 1988, eleven of the original twenty-two activists are found guilty of the murder of the policeman. Nkoli is acquitted. The sentences of the remaining prisoners are overturned following an appeal to the Supreme Court, and they are all finally released.

Anyone attempting to unravel the events that took place behind those prison walls by reading Nkoli's letters from that period will be disappointed. They're held by GALA (Gay and Lesbian Memory in Action), the South African organisation entrusted with the archives of the country's gay activist movement, but the letters from prisoner X39/85 reveal very little. Those written to his partner Roy Shepherd contain hardly any reference to the fierce discussions taking place in prison. The same goes for the letters exchanged between Nkoli and Carolyn Nichols, the girlfriend of his cellmate Gcina Malindi. Without exception, they describe at great length prison life, as well as the considerable interest Nkoli has in events taking place in the wider world – amongst his family, his partner and his friends.

At the start of his detention, he imagines attending a party and describes in detail what he would have worn. He then goes on to hint at his downcast frame of mind. In August 1985, he writes to Roy that he has been unable to unearth the prison numbers of his fellow inmates. Shepherd had wanted to send each of them a letter. The correspondence between the two is clearly frosty; "for reasons that I cannot go into, I am not accepted here for who I am." He considers distancing himself from the group and standing trial alone. Malinda eventually persuades him not to. "He begged me not to go it alone," Nkoli writes later in the month. However, other letters recall the huge amount of post he receives from outside South Africa that he considers a massive boost to his morale. They contain expressions of solidarity after gay friends have spread the word of his arrest and anti-apartheid groups and gay movements from around the world have called for a show of support. Further *Nkolia* has been dug up by Anthony Manion, a hugely helpful archivist, but little of consequence has been found relating to the prison discussions. There are newspaper reports from the trial and photos showing a strident and broadly smiling Nkoli just after his release. There are also countless interviews from a later date in which he speaks more openly, as well as *Simon and Me*, the impressive documentary by filmmaker Beverley Ditsie. GALA also holds the original manuscript of a play that recounts the story of his life and which played to packed houses in Johannesburg.

There's a simple explanation for a lack of any substantial evidence from Nkoli's correspondence of the discussions taking place during those prison years: any direct reference would have immediately been picked up by the prison authorities, as all of the incoming and outgoing post was controlled and censored. But Nkoli also wanted to prevent the underlying differences in the group from becoming known to their accusers. It would, without question, have been used to undermine the group and create further tensions between them.

Nkoli's often re-told story isn't the only proof of the altercations that took place during those prison years. Shortly after his untimely death in November 1998 at the age of forty-one from an AIDS related illness, a memorial service takes place at St. Mary's Cathedral, the Anglican church in the centre of Johannesburg. Mosiuoa Lekota is one of the speakers. By this time, he is the chair of the ANC, and a year later he will become defence minister in Thabo Mbeki's government. It's a far cry from the days in his youth when he was given the nickname 'Terror' because of the reckless way he played on the football field. His eulogy praises Nkoli as "a man of principle who was able to keep up his spirits when everyone else was losing theirs". Lekota recalls their days in captivity together and touches on a delicate subject: "Young men have sexual longings. These can't just be switched off at will in prison. In detention I only knew men who would do whatever was necessary to relieve themselves of their sexual frustrations. But Simon told me that there were other men who call themselves 'gay' and who form relationships with other men on equal terms."

Lekota's speech recollects how the white minority government sought all manner of ways to destroy their political opponents and to undermine their credibility as 'freedom fighters'. The fear that this had instilled poisoned the discussions over homosexuality that he'd had with Nkoli. "Until one day I eat a 'twin banana'," Lekota proclaims. He pauses for a moment before explaining what he means: "No, not two bananas independent of each other that happened to be joined. No, these were two complete bananas that had grown together within the same skin. I immediately thought: if Simon is gay, why can't I just enjoy his company as much as everyone else's?"

Of course, one can easily ridicule Lekota's ham-fisted attempt to understand Nkoli's sexuality, and opponents of equal rights for homosexuals are quick to interpret his words as an attempt to justify the unjustifiable, but it's clear that Lekota is speaking from the heart.

Lekota confesses that he now "felt bad" about his revulsion of his comrade's sexual preferences and his reluctance to accept it. But these prejudices disappeared once it dawned upon him "that there was, within our struggle for democracy, another struggle going on that is of no less importance and which sooner or later would come to the fore". It therefore went without saying, according to Lekota, that the question of equal rights for everyone, regardless of sexual orientation, had to be resolved as soon as the foundations for a new constitution had been laid down.

A week later, Lekota also speaks at Nkoli's funeral in Sebokeng, the township of his youth. He reiterates his words from the memorial service: "It was unthinkable after the release of Nelson Mandela and the decriminalisation of the ANC at the beginning of the 1990s that we would have gone to the negotiating table without discussing the rights of our homosexual comrades." Lekota is joined at the funeral by a number of his former co-defendants, such as Popo Molefe, now the premier of the North-West province, and Frank Chikane, the general secretary of the Council of Churches, and who a year later is to become the director general of the presidency under Thabo Mbeki. Tom Manthata is also present. Years later, when we're researching information on what exactly went on in the prison during their internment, he tells us, in his office at the South African Human Rights Commission, that he can remember nothing of the highly charged discussions that had taken place there. Yes, he knew that Simon was gay: "For that reason he received expressions of affection from around the world," he scoffs. "But to make so much of it now..."

*

The *pink archives* have been housed at the University of Witwatersrand in the centre of Johannesburg since 1997. They form a *mer à boire* for researchers, journalists and anyone wanting to know more about the lives of South Africa's LGBTs under apartheid and thereafter. Thanks to the detective work of employees and hundreds of donations in the form of diaries, photos, newspaper cuttings and filmed or recorded interviews, the collection is unparalleled anywhere in Africa. The relative openness that quickly developed after Mandela's release gave members of GALA the opportunity to publicize, via the media, their wish to collect historical material relating to their cause. Such an approach is still unthinkable in many other African countries due to the fact that gay activists must often operate in covert networks — it's prudent to destroy anything that might be seen as incriminating evidence.

GALA's archivist leads us into the catacombs of the university where the archives are stored in row upon row of cabinets. The temperature is carefully controlled to preserve the films, negatives, photographs, and countless T-shirts, banners, badges and protest boards. It's a collection that might strike Western visitors as a throwback to the 1970s, but these archives contain the history of a movement that reached its peak in the 1990s. However, the earliest material dates back to long before the beginning of the apartheid era in 1948. It relates to research carried out by filmmaker Jack Lewis who bequeathed his collection to GALA. It contains references to the Cape *Bandietenrollen* – the centuries old register of criminal cases kept at the National Archives in Cape Town. From here, the story of Rijkhaart Jacobz and Klaas Blank has been unearthed. Jacobz was a redhead from Rotterdam who was charged in 1713 in the Netherlands with "a crime that could not be named". He was banished to Robben Island and the so-called 'Bandit House', a building made from mud and twigs with a view over the Indian Ocean.

Shortly after his arrival, he was joined by four others: Manaij van Bougies, Klaas van Kus Malaba, Petrus Malgas and Klaas Blank. They were all Khoi, the original inhabitants of the Cape, and were each banished to Robben Island for fifty years for crimes relating to theft. It was here in the limestone quarry that Blank, a small, coloured man in his twenties, and Jacobz got to know each other. It seems that it wasn't long before the two confessed their love for each other. One can only speculate as to how they were able to continue their tryst, but it seems that Klaas was supplying the guards with the highly popular *dagga* (marijuana) and perhaps it was for this reason that the two were allowed to build their own hut on Robben Island's beach. They lived there together for the next twenty years.

Sergeant Scholtz was the prison colony's supervisor and was himself involved in a relationship with a freed female slave. It's clear that he was turning a blind eye to the couple's relationship. When Manaij van Bougies, one day in 1735, mislaid his fishing net, rumours soon circulated that Rijkhaart Jacobz was the culprit. When Van Bougies confronted him, the Rotterdammer is said to have dropped his trousers and stroked his penis. It was this incident that led to a slave named Augustijn Matthisz recalling something that had happened eleven years before. He'd seen the couple "guilty of performing a terrible sin" in their hut. They all rushed to Sergeant Scholtz to tell him everything that had happened. The supervisor showed no interest. However, his retirement shortly afterwards changed everything. The men grabbed their chance. Scholtz's successor was more attentive to their stories. Godlieb Willer was a deeply religious man and immediately went to work bringing Jacobz to book. Jacobz initially denied the accusations, claiming he was drunk when Matthisz had seen him with Blank. He was only naked because his trousers had fallen down. It took a heavy thrashing with the *sjambok* for him to confess. "Don't hit me! I did it. Send me to the courtroom," Jacobz is said to have cried.

"The prisoner has pleaded guilty to all charges," reports the *Bandietenrollen*. On 18 August 1735, Jacobz and Blank were both sentenced to death. A few days later, they were chained to each other wearing only their prison trousers and taken out to sea where they were thrown to the sharks. This deeply moving story inspired Jack Lewis to make *Proteus* — just one of many productions with a homosexual theme that has come out of South Africa since the end of apartheid.

The Man Who Drove with Mandela is an intriguing documentary by the South African journalist Mark Gevisser that was shown at the Cannes Film Festival at the end of the 1990s. It tells the story of Cecil Williams, a white, gay theatre director and communist who became involved in the fight against apartheid, and was Nelson Mandela's personal chauffeur in the years before his arrest. The film shows how Williams emigrated from England to South Africa in 1928 to teach theatre. It wasn't long before he became active in the anti-fascist *Sprinkbok Legion*, a movement that successfully lobbied for South Africa not to take the side of the Nazis in the lead up to the Second World War. He made his name as a theatre director who gave as many roles to black actors as to white ones. His parties were legendary, attracting the likes of the American comic Danny Kaye and the British classical actor Laurence Olivier, but his involvement with the anti-apartheid movement during this period is not widely known. Gevisser's film tells Williams' story using the accounts of eyewitnesses and historical footage; a history that ends in 1962 with the arrest of both himself and Mandela. Williams was released after a brief detention but returned to England shortly afterwards, where he remained until his death in 1979.

In the thought-provoking docudrama *Property of the State*, the writer and filmmaker Gerald Kraak, who died in 2014, reconstructs the history of homosexuals serving in the army under apartheid. It's known that at least nine hundred men and women were given electric shock treatment during the 1970s and 1980s in an attempt to alter their sexual preferences. The man responsible was Colonel Aubrey Levin who emigrated to Canada after the collapse of the apartheid regime and was able to avoid the hearings of the Truth and Reconciliation Commission that began its work in 1995. Levin became a professor in clinical psychology at the medical department of the University of Calgary, and never had to answer for his actions. Ironically, in 2013 Levin was found guilty of sexually assaulting three of his male patients and sentenced to five years in prison.

There is an enormous collection in GALA's DVD archive. Hundreds of hours of film bear testament to the seemingly endless exploration of the rich and sometimes deeply moving gay life in South Africa. And the telling of these stories is no longer the preserve of white filmmakers. In 2011, Zanele Muholi's documentary film *Difficult Love* was shown at numerous international film festivals. It's a fierce indictment of the extreme animosity that's still directed at black lesbian women in South Africa, but also suggests that public opinion is gradually beginning to change. The film was financed by the country's public broadcaster, although there was considerable hesitation and delay before it was broadcast in South Africa itself. Ditsie's *Simon & I*, as well as Mpumi Njinges's *My Son, the Bride,* which follows the preparations for one of the first gay marriages in South Africa, and the same director's *Everything Must Come to Light,* about lesbian traditional healers (*sangomas*), all attracted considerable attention in the country. It came just in time for Njinges to enjoy the success, as this talented, young filmmaker died in 2002 from an AIDS related disease. The annual, highly popular and talked about *Out of Africa International Film Festival* is no longer restricted to screening international productions thanks to the emergence of these home-grown gay-themed films.

GALA's endless newspaper cuttings are a mine of useful information that helps bring a forgotten history back to life. In clippings from the 1930s, we come across an article with the heading "Dutch sailor prostitution ring" about male sex workers in Cape Town. Other documents and articles give an insight into gangs such as the notorious *409s*, and to the drag culture in the mineworkers' hostels where men are known to have dressed as women. There are fascinating photographs that show a lively gay subculture in Cape Town's District Six in the very heart of the city – a vibrant, multicultural community that was later completely destroyed when the apartheid leaders ordered the bulldozers to move in. There is also footage of the Hope and Unity Metropolitan Community Church in Johannesburg, a church founded in the mid-1990s and a clear reminder of how important faith still is in the life of young African gays and lesbians.

Thanks to GALA's unrivalled enthusiasm for collecting, it's possible to find almost anything dating from the 1980s onwards relating to the gay movement, from demonstrations and petitions to meetings, lobbying and internal fights. The relatively short history of South Africa's gay activism can be seamlessly pieced together by sifting through this valuable resource. However, the relevance of various actions, and which of them should be given most prominence, is still being disputed. After all, the success of the country's LGBT movement has many fathers and mothers. More on that later.

*

As he has promised, Simon Nkoli, shortly after his release from prison in 1988, founds a gay movement. He calls it the "Gays and Lesbians of the Witwatersrand" (GLOW), and it allows him to draw a line under his troubled relationship with the predominantly white membership of the Gay Association of South Africa (GASA) that he joined in 1983. It was within this organisation that he'd started the so-called Saturday Group, the very first black gay organisation of its kind in Africa – giving the chance for GASA, which had been conspicuously white in its outlook, to show that it represents *all* of the country's homosexuals, and to give a voice to the lesbians, bisexuals and transgender people who had, until that point, garnered very little attention. However, it loses all credibility following its reaction to Nkoli's arrest and imprisonment. GASA's stance is that one doesn't get involved in politics. This standpoint is scrutinised at an ILGA (now the International Lesbian, Gay, Bisexual, Trans and Intersex Association) conference in Copenhagen in 1986, a meeting of representatives of gay organisations from around the world. Delegates from GASA refuse to be drawn into any discussion over insinuations that they have failed to show solidarity with Nkoli. According to GASA, the matter is simple – no support can be forthcoming because Nkoli has been accused of involvement in 'terrorist activities'. The conference members appear to concur: a motion to suspend GASA is overwhelmingly rejected. GASA's president James Willett-Clark interprets the result as a defeat for the 'anti-South Africa forces'. It must have been music to the ears of the apartheid regime's leaders. Whilst the white minority government is being further isolated internationally, ILGA choses to continue working with GASA. The importance it lends to solidarity within the international gay movement (predominantly white males) is seemingly greater than its resistance to apartheid.

However, GASA does subsequently make attempts to improve its tarnished image. It announces it will conduct research into the consequences for homosexuality under apartheid. Whether this actually takes place is open to conjecture as the results of this research never see the light of day. The board of GASA also offers its apologies to Nkoli for assuming his guilt before any verdict has been delivered in court. In fact, these sentiments harden feelings against them, as it suggests a trust in a legal system that relies on racist laws and which criminalises practically every form of resistance to the white minority government. GASA is finally expelled from ILGA in 1987. It's the same year the state of emergency in South Africa is extended for a third time. Thousands of political activists are in prison, disappearances and kidnappings are the order of the day, and attacks on the exiled community in neighbouring countries are commonplace. The press is silenced, whilst numerous organisations are declared illegal. The reality of the situation is slowly beginning to dawn on ILGA's members.

The increasing and escalating repression in the latter part of the 1980s forms the backdrop to a discrete but growing multi-racial LGBT movement. There is a subtle irony in the fact that the white rulers, who are brought up under the influence of the distinctly anti-homosexual teachings of the Dutch Reformed Church, have their hands too full with other political matters to expend too much energy hounding the homosexual community. The strain is beginning to show on a political system that the United Nations has declared a 'crime against humanity'. It means that Nkoli has enough breathing space to recruit new members to GLOW with little outside interference, and to take a more activist approach to gay rights.

As the conflict between supporters and opponents of apartheid is moving perilously close to civil war, high-level meetings are taking place with great secrecy between representatives from both sides. We now know that the ANC leaders Thabo Mkebi and Jacob Zuma hold a number of covert meetings in a hotel room in the Swiss capital Bern with employees of the South African intelligence service. At the end of the 1980s, Mbeki travels to Washington to dine with members of the secret Afrikaner Brotherhood, the most important think-tank linked to the white minority government and which maintains an iron grip on the appointments made under the apartheid system. Nelson Mandela, still imprisoned on Robben Island, is now known to have held talks from 1987 onwards with members of the South African cabinet, especially the justice minister Kobie Coetsee. An increasing number of the Afrikaner establishment – artists, businessmen, and representatives of churches and cultural organisations – all take part in meetings with prominent ANC members in places as diverse as Dakar, Paris and Harare. As the anti-apartheid rhetoric grows ever stronger, and the call for sanctions and a boycott of South Africa increases, the ANC makes the calculation that it would be wise to prepare for negotiations with an enemy that they know will eventually have no other choice but to negotiate with them. In order to be thoroughly prepared for any talks, the ANC works hard on devising various transitional models and blueprints for a democratic South Africa.

And whilst Nkoli is busy concentrating his efforts into shaping grass roots activism in Johannesburg, gay ANC supporters in Cape Town are involved in behind-the-scenes lobbying in an attempt to influence the debate. They make contact with prominent ANC activists such as the lawyer Albie Sachs, who has survived an assassination attempt whilst in exile in Mozambique, and law professor Kader Asmal. Both men are considered important influences in shaping the course of any future South African constitution. Church leaders such as Archbishop Desmond Tutu, the pastor Allan Boesak and the Muslim theologian Farid Esack, who are all playing a prominent role in the fight against apartheid, make no secret of their support for the lobbying taking place. It's clear that gay rights are on the ANC's political agenda from an early stage.

An incident occurs in 1987 that's manna from heaven for those gay activists determined to stir up the debate. An interview appears in the British magazine *Capital Gay* with ANC board members Ruth Mompati and Solly Smith in which they both declare that equal rights for gays and lesbians are not on the agenda. Mompati states that the idea of a specific group being singled out for special attention is abhorrent and sweeps aside any suggestion that minorities could have their own organisations. "We don't have a policy on flower sellers either," she says in her interview with the activist Peter Tatchell. Solly Smith agrees wholeheartedly. It later becomes known that during this period he is acting as an informant for the apartheid regime's police force. The interview sparks a storm of protest from Western LGBT movements which are becoming increasingly involved with the struggle against apartheid. The stream of letters and expressions of disgust that flood in, also from anti-apartheid organisations, strikes a chord with an ANC that understands how important the support of these groups is for keeping its cause in the spotlight outside of South Africa.

Of course, it's easy to condemn Mompati and Smith's statements. They are undoubtedly homophobic, and distaste for a 'deviant' sexual preference was certainly playing a role. But it's also possible that a life in exile creates its own distortions and frustrations. As the years go by, they may long for their own culturally specific surroundings, instead of what they may perceive as a strange and individualistic society full of radical 'queers and dykes'. But it's equally plausible that those who consider themselves representatives of a disenfranchised black South African *majority* may instinctively go on the defensive as soon as any *minority* starts demanding equal rights. After all, they had been suppressed for so long by a white minority that considered itself superior, and which allocated all sorts of privileges based primarily on the basis of specific characteristics. It's possible that these ANC'ers thought: never again!

The official response from Thabo Mbeki, who is heading the information department of ANC operations in exile, is both business-like and to the point. A month after the publication of the magazine article, he writes a letter to the same publication distancing himself from his two colleagues. Mbeki describes sexual preference as a 'private matter' in which one should not interfere. It suggests he is not yet willing to fully endorse the calls for a specific clause to be written into the constitution guaranteeing the right to be free from discrimination on the grounds of sexual orientation. He does however, emphasize that he wants to "eliminate any doubt about the intention of the ANC to grant equal rights in a future, democratic and non-sexist South Africa to everyone". A self-evident standpoint perhaps, but a courageous one too, as his words put a strain on the otherwise friendly relations the ANC has with other liberation movements elsewhere in Africa.

*

In February 1990, the South African President F.W. de Klerk announces the decriminalisation of the ANC and releases Nelson Mandela. The state of emergency that has been in place since 1985 is partially lifted. All political prisoners are to be freed, and thousands of South Africans living in exile can return home. The strict censorship laws are softened. The white minority government is clearly in deep trouble. It has been unable to break the resistance movement with heavy-handed repression, international banks are no longer prepared to extend loans, white intellectuals and, increasingly, the country's 'captains of industry' are speaking out against apartheid ideology. There seems to be a realisation that the suppression of the black majority is no longer serving their own interest but, on the contrary, is adversely affecting it. Western governments feel compelled to step up sanctions against Pretoria, under pressure from the rapidly growing solidarity movement. There is almost universal agreement that Mandela and the thousands of other political prisoners should be released.

Despite all this, the government is far from throwing in the towel. It still has complete control over the secret services, and the government departments are still run by those loyal to the regime. Western leaders like the British Prime Minister Margaret Thatcher and US President Ronald Reagan are still wary of speaking out wholeheartedly against apartheid, sharing the same fear as the white leaders in Pretoria of the 'black peril' and the 'red peril' – and South Africa's collapse into the hands of 'international communists'. But the international situation is rapidly changing. The Berlin wall has fallen and the introduction of glasnost and perestroika is being hailed as a new era in the Soviet Union's chequered history. It's against this backdrop that De Klerk believes there is a strong chance he'll be able to introduce changes without having to give up power completely. This misplaced scenario does not include a transitional period culminating in a fully democratic system. On the contrary, his plan involves negotiating a settlement for a federal South Africa in which the white minority would keep certain privileges. De Klerk wants a senate based on ethnic representation and in which the white minority would have as much influence as the black majority. He also wants a rotating presidency. No matter how great any electoral mandate would be for a black president, after one or two years he must make way for a leader from another section of the country's population. From the middle of the 1980s onwards, the heads of the police and the army develop a strategy designed to sow discord and distrust amongst the black minority, and to undermine Mandela and his ANC movement. With this in mind, they hand weapons to Inkatha, the predominantly Zulu backed movement that feels threatened by the massive popularity of the ANC. Members of Inkatha are trained by the military in secret locations, whilst the intelligence services are personally involved in a number of clashes and the fuelling of violent conflict. Shortly after his release, Mandela accuses De Klerk of failing to take action against this so-called 'third force' operating from within the intelligence services and which has the specific intention of preventing the ANC from winning a majority in any future democratic election. Journalists and political commentators react with scepticism to the claims, but the existence of such a clandestine force is confirmed in later years during the hearings of the Truth and Reconciliation Commission.

De Klerk gambles on being able to direct the course of the ensuing changes. No conditions for the release of Mandela are set down, nor are any conditions set for the decriminalisation of his movement – up to that moment, it had been demanded that they lay down their weapons first; but De Klerk thinks he will be able to control the subsequent developments, and to a large extent shape the course of events. The aim is to somehow share power whilst ensuring that the full aspirations of the black majority are contained, allowing them some representation without unduly upsetting the existing power structure.

It's a fanciful notion. De Klerk underestimates the effect of the changes he's unleashed. Thirty years after the British Prime Minister Harold Macmillan makes his famous "winds of change" speech calling for the South African parliament in Cape Town to rethink its policies, the gusts of wind that have been gradually gaining strength finally start to blow things over. The floodgates are open. People are no longer willing to be fobbed off with half-hearted measures and a few token blacks in high positions giving an impression of a more equal society. They want the end of special privileges for whites and the creation of a 'one person, one vote' electoral system in which the majority vote wins – *Amandla Ngwethu*, power to the people! The genie is out of the bottle and the longing for a free, non-racial and non-sexist South Africa is finally beginning to take shape. Gay activists in Johannesburg and Cape Town are determined not to be left on the sidelines, and, following De Klerk's speech on 2 February 1990, sense the chance to place their own demands on the negotiating table.

*

It is October 1990, just eight months after Mandela's release from prison, and the first Gay and Lesbian Pride March is taking place through the streets of Johannesburg. It consists initially of about two hundred, mostly young people, but as the march progresses the numbers grow. By the time the crowd has reached its final destination in a park, it has swelled to an estimated one thousand people. The march starts with many of the participants covering their heads with brown paper bags, but the enthusiasm and the excitement generated by this inaugural Pride March leads to many of them revealing their faces. It has become a collective 'coming-out'. The name they give to the march shows a direct kinship with similar events elsewhere in the world, but the concept of 'a march', in this instance, is to display a partisanship with the anti-apartheid liberation movement that has helped instil an irreversible desire for change with marches, boycotts and activism . The Gay Pride march has the feel of a protest against apartheid – the *toyi toyi* can be heard in the crowd – a rhythmic chanting and stomping of feet that is often used during political demonstrations as a sign of dissent; marshals ensure the procession proceeds in an orderly fashion; and the numerous transvestites who head the cortege make it abundantly clear to the many onlookers that this is no ordinary protest.

Simon Nkoli sets the tone with a speech before the march begins. "I am fighting for the abolition of apartheid," he says, "And I'm fighting for the right to be free from discrimination on the grounds of my sexuality. The two are inextricably linked. It's not possible to fight one without fighting the other, or to place them in order of importance. I cannot be free as a black man, as long as I am not free as a gay man." It is met with a rapturous applause. Speeches made by Edwin Cameron and Beverley Ditsie also make a big impression. Cameron is a lawyer who in 2009 will take his seat as a judge in the Constitutional Court, after being nominated by President Zuma. He later recollects the deep unease many of them felt in the lead up to the Gay Pride march. Was it wise to put one's head above the parapet? Would it provoke a violent backlash and quash any hope before their cause had gathered any momentum? Their fears were unwarranted; once the march is underway, any doubts are quickly swept aside.

But Beverley Ditsie, who joined GLOW shortly after its inception, remembers some anxious moments. Writing about her experiences in those early days, she describes how, a few days after she was shown on national television giving one of the speeches, around twenty boys turned up at her house in Soweto, "to teach me a lesson". "They want to fix me," she writes – they had come to rape her. Her grandmother blocked the doorway and prevented them from entering. According to Ditsie, "the iron bar my grandmother held in her hand they mistook for a gun." The boys left, but she didn't dare show her face for weeks afterwards. "I then realised that I had gained the support of my whole family, and not just that of my grandmother," she concludes.

There is also one other deeply moving speech from that first Gay and Lesbian Pride march. A pastor from the Dutch/German Reformed Church speaks directly to his Lord and Master, and then announces to him that he is leaving the church. It leaves a big impression on those present.

This very first openly gay expression of solidarity and activism receives considerable attention in the media, and it's no surprise that the *drag queens* dominate the coverage, to the disappointment of some of the activists. They feel it gives a distorted image of the movement, and in subsequent marches the organisers attempt to keep this section of the gay community out of the spotlight. It's a hopeless task, even more difficult than amending the explicitly anti-gay South African laws. In the years to come, the *fopdossers,* as they are called in Afrikaans, would be as conspicuous as ever at the front of the marches.

At the very end of the first Pride march comes the call to 'take the hand of the person standing next to you'. And then 'hug them and give them a big kiss on the mouth!' It's meant as a wry joke, and also a provocation. The crowd, a diverse mix of the South African population, immediately does what has been asked. It becomes a multicultural 'kiss and make-up' – a reconciliation. For many of those taking part it is a truly earth shattering experience. After all, this is a generation that has grown up with segregation and 'whites only' notices and the Immorality Law that made extramarital sex between blacks and whites illegal. This fledgling new movement has, in one communal kiss, become a trailblazer. Different groups, that have been deeply divided for so long, put aside their differences and show the time is ripe for change. It demonstrates that the end result of any high level negotiations (which in practice takes four more years of heated and sometimes dramatic discussion) must ultimately be all about living together as one. And so, on this South African spring day in early October, everything seems possible.

And then events take on a momentum of their own. After the initial 'talks about talks', official negotiations on the future democratic course of the country begin in December 1991. The membership of GLOW grows rapidly, especially in the townships around Johannesburg. The organisation offers training and *Miss GLOW* contests. It's also active in campaigns to open up 'white only' gay venues to homosexuals from all races. Nkoli uses his position as advisor to the Township AIDS Project in Soweto to initiate the first 'condom droppings'. The AIDS virus, unlike in the West, is not predominantly spreading within the gay community. However, South African gay campaigners, as in the West, are at the forefront of raising awareness of the dangers of the disease. Gay movements are also taking shape in other cities such as Cape Town, Pretoria and Durban. Activists create a network in which a number of influential spokespersons develop contacts with negotiators from the ANC, the ruling National Party and other groups. It includes Edwin Cameron and the two Cape activists Zackie Achmat and Sheila Lapinsky. A lobbyist is employed who is paid using a secret fund set up by wealthy white gays and lesbians in the 1970s in reaction to a rumour that had been circulating that the country's rulers were proposing to strengthen the anti-gay laws even further. The fund was originally intended to finance any possible legal action, but the rumours proved unfounded and the money remained unused.

The lobbying and activism claims a first success with its involvement in ensuring that 'the right to be free from discrimination on the grounds of sexual orientation' is to be included in a transitional constitution.

During this time, the Pride marches have become big annual events, attracting thousands and subsequently tens of thousands of participants.

The first democratic national elections take place in April 1994. Most of De Klerk's original plans for the white minority to maintain its grip on power have fallen by the wayside. Every vote counts. A Truth and Reconciliation Commission will delve into apartheid's human right's violations. Mandela has already let it be known that a 'government of national unity' will be formed of which the former rulers will also be a part. It has also been agreed that officials who worked under the apartheid system will not automatically lose their jobs. As expected, the ANC wins a landslide victory with more than sixty per cent of the vote. The next month, the National Assembly formally elects Mandela as the country's first black president. The country breaths a collective sigh of relief. Tensions had been running high in the preceding years, but the transition has ultimately been a relatively peaceful one.

But there is still work to be done. Gay activists must ensure the new government will be true to its word and that the definitive constitution will contain everything expected of it. A National Coalition of Gay and Lesbian Equality is formed made up of members from a range of different local organisations. An office is set up in Johannesburg that becomes the main operating centre for the likes of Zackie Achmat, Simon Nkoli, the well-respected lawyer Phumzile Mthetwa, and Mazibuko Jara, a communist and heterosexual mining engineer who is sympathetic to their cause. Achmat is seen as a brilliant strategist who in later years founds the Treatment Action Campaign that is to play an important role in urging the government to change tack and implement a credible AIDS policy. The group is determined to keep a high profile and its members are often guests on radio and television talk shows and quoted in national newspapers and magazines. The debate over homosexuality becomes one of the main topics of discussion relating to the new constitution. The president himself shows an active interest and in the spring of 1995 welcomes a delegation that includes the British actor Ian McKellen, who is on tour in the country at the time, as well as Nkoli and Mthetwa. Mandela lets them know of his support of LGBT rights, but also emphasises the difficulty that many of his compatriots are having with the idea. "Strong leaders aren't afraid of leading their troops," Mandela is quoted as saying, but he also calls on them to engage in discussion, and to be patient in tackling widely held prejudices.

Meanwhile, the LGBT movement in South Africa is blossoming. The number of organisations grows, together with the membership, and the first 'gay church' opens its doors in Johannesburg. Cape Town starts its own Pride march and a 'pink film festival' is launched in all of the country's most important cities. To cap it all, on 10 December 1996, a joint meeting of the elected representatives adopts the new constitution by a large majority and a new Constitutional Court is set up to ensure its implementation.

In the years that follow, many of the anti-gay provisions imbedded in various laws are removed. Gays and lesbians gain equal pension rights. Adoption for homosexual couples is permitted. In 2006, South Africa becomes the first country on the continent to legalise same-sex marriage and only the third to do so in the world.

In these crucial years, during which South Africa changes beyond imagination, gay activists work unrelenting hours to fulfil their ambitions. Their lives are being devoted to achieving goals that few dared to think possible. But the years of struggle begin to take their toll and fatigue sets in. Many no longer have the energy to work day and night on a cause they feel has been won, and redirect it into artistic ambitions, studying, or simply maintaining a relationship. There are also those like Zackie Achmat, who in the late 1990s becomes involved in another struggle of paramount importance. The Cape activist has been diagnosed with HIV infection and is outraged by the shameful and peculiar unwillingness of Mandela's successor Thabo Mbeki to fight AIDS with all the means possible.

Emotions also run high amongst black gay activists over the feeling that some of their white counterparts are less than enthusiastic in accepting them as equal partners in the struggle for equality. They feel there is, at times, an unwillingness to share the stage and give important roles to their black compatriots. The multicultural kiss at the end of the first Pride march is being viewed as a one-off, as white South Africans within the LGBT movement often cling to their positions of power just as much as those in other sections of society. As a consequence, LGBT associations become too detached from the reality of everyday life for ordinary black South Africans, and two decades after the sweeping changes that have shaken the country, the remnants of apartheid are still clearly visible. Certainly a new black middle-class has emerged, but the overwhelming majority still live in the townships, often a great distance from the city centres. Despite all the undoubted change and progress that has taken place, a lack of amenities still prevails. Government spending has been more fairly distributed, but healthcare and education in areas where whites predominate still tend to be better equipped. One of the unfortunate characteristics of organisations with a majority of white employees is that they consider their work in the black townships to be 'outreach' programmes, a sort of charity aimed at the disadvantaged. In 2001, staff members of the Lesbian and Gay Equality Project (LGEP) – the new name of the National Coalition – are criticised for allegedly ignoring complaints from black gay men relating to the door policy of a number of venues. Rumours are flying within the gay scene in Jo'burg of people being refused entry. Sometimes the reason stated is that it is 'membership only', on other occasions a dress code is enforced – certain persons are not deemed suitably attired to be allowed in. The accusations are that the venue's owners still favour a predominantly white-only clientele. LGEP refuse to take action, giving the impression that it is 'in bed' with the proprietors, and leading to a distrust developing amongst its black constituency. There is a feeling that

LGEP is willing only to pay lip service to the idea of a full black representation within its movement, and is always at pains to stress that the recruitment of blacks is not easy, that there aren't enough blacks qualified for high level positions — 'there's still a long way to go', LGEP staff stresses. At times, it seems to be suggesting that it would be irresponsible to leave the organisation in the hands of people who couldn't be trusted with the accounting or to keep track of the flow of money. Those organisations that are black from inception, or have been through a thorough transformation, are amused by the inferences and look on with a sense of *schadenfreude* as LGEP subsequently tries to deal with a seemingly endless stream of controversies. Evidence comes to light of financial mismanagement. Its relationship with other organisations is put under considerable strain.

There is also frustration building up over the under-representation of women on the boards and management of many gay organisations. Transgender people, for their part, are successful in their attempt to place the T into LGBT, but the discrimination they have been facing is, for many years, seemingly ignored.

Despite all these setbacks, during the period around the new millennium, many new associations are established. In 2000, the daily web magazine *Behind the Mask* (BTM) begins its coverage of developments across Africa that relate to homosexuality. *The Mask* also creates a platform for the massive creative developments taking place, tapping into the huge potential of new technology that's giving everyone the opportunity to tell their story. Its headquarters is an office space made available by Johannesburg city council and is situated in the 'Women's Gaol', the former women's prison where anti-apartheid freedom fighters such as Albertina Sisulu and Winnie Mandela had been locked up. The building is part of a large complex on Constitution Hill that includes a museum and the offices of the Gender Commission, as well as the courtroom of the new Constitutional Court. *Behind the Mask* closes its operations in 2010. These days, almost all gay movements across Africa rely on websites to inform their members of initiatives and developments, and use Facebook and Twitter to keep activists in touch with each other.

The Constitutional Court, as has already been mentioned, has played a hugely influential role in the liberation struggle of the LGBT movement. However, there are those who point to the difference that exists between the legal rights of homosexuals, and the reality under which they live. People are beginning to wonder whether the rejoicing has been a little premature. The dramatic increase in violence against lesbians, the so-called 'hate crimes', especially in the first decade of this century, has left some gay activists describing the hard-fought rights they have won as something of a pyrrhic victory. The alarm bells are first sounded by Zanele Muholi and her then partner Donna Smith. Muholi is struck by the fact that many of her black lesbian friends have no knowledge of the contents of the new constitution and what it means for them particularly. The daily reality of many lesbians is one of marginalisation and violence. In the townships especially, some young men, seeing the rise of women in politics, the law and business, are consequently taking out their frustrations on lesbians in their own neighbourhoods. These lesbians, in turn, are becoming bolder in speaking out, but this increasing visibility of lesbian women has also led to a growing vulnerability. It's a painful irony, and one that Muholi and Smith are quick to draw attention to with their 'Rose has Thorns' anti-hate crime campaign, a pointed warning to the perpetrators. The Johannesburg based 'Forum for the Empowerment of Women' is established on the back of this, made up of predominantly black lesbians. It quickly wins the support of local organisations, which in stark contrast to the earlier years of gay activism, are now being led by women.

It's a sad fact that the most liberated country in Africa also boasts the highest levels of violence against gays and lesbians. There's now a yawning gap between expectation and reality. While the South African parliament prepares a new law against hate crimes, the violence continues. However, gay activists are claiming a victory of sorts with the fact that this specific form of violent crime has been defined, and that the perpetrators face the prospect of longer jail sentences.

The lawyer Edwin Cameron calls the homosexual clause in the constitution a 'freedom bonus'. This rather ambiguous term highlights the fact that the clause was included despite garnering little support from the population at large. It shows what can be achieved by the persistent and well-organised lobbying of a small group – in contrast to the long, drawn-out deliberations characteristic of a process that is broadly supported by the population, such as the case in the Netherlands. Whilst the new constitution has breathed new life into the anti-racist aspirations of the great majority of South Africans, it has not yet inspired a similar awakening in the way LGBT people are viewed by ordinary citizens. The same goes, but perhaps to a lesser degree, for the way women's rights in the constitution have been interpreted and accepted; see, for example, the subsequent legalisation of abortion. Equally, the abolition of the death penalty is highly unlikely to survive the result of any referendum on the subject. Shortly after Nelson Mandela's inauguration as president, he warns gay activists that many South Africans, regardless of the colour of their skin, are conservative by nature. Research has tended to confirm this time and again, whether it is Whites, Indians, Coloureds, Jews or Blacks.

Despite all this, many gay activists believe that the momentum is flowing in the right direction. They cite, as examples, how all the anti-gay legislation has been extinguished from the law books, and the rise of gay characters in television soap operas. *Isidingo*, a daily soap produced by the Dutch production company Endemol for South African national television, includes a storyline involving a gay marriage. The annual Pride events continue to celebrate the newly acquired rights. There is a pervading spirit of elation and triumph. When a US based book appears on the shelves around the turn of the century with a very clear anti-gay stance, the staff members of the National Coalition gay movement weigh up the pros and cons of demanding its banning. It seems as though some activists see the constitution as the *de facto* State Bible – the word of law is God and that is sufficient in itself. However, when they realise their organisation would gain the rather dubious reputation of being the very first to call for a book to be banned since the ending of apartheid, they wisely reconsider their position. In the end, it supports a legal action brought by a private individual. The judge's subsequent ruling states that a warning should appear on the book's cover due to its controversial content, but it has acquired a lot more attention and publicity because of the court proceedings.

Nearly two decades after the adoption of the new constitution, there remains an inconsistency and ambivalence to the LGBT struggle in South Africa – and at times an outright contradiction. In the guestbook of a small exhibition about homosexuality in the Apartheid Museum in Johannesburg, hundreds of school children write the most candid and straightforward messages against discrimination. The younger generation seems to have shrugged off the inherent prejudices of its elders. Former political prisoners, who now conduct guided tours around Robben Island, proudly show visitors the little church where the country's very first gay marriage took place. South Africa's representatives at the UN play a key role in gathering support for the international organisation's ground breaking call for its members to condemn any form of discrimination towards gays and lesbians, transgender people and bisexuals, as well as other sexual minorities. Following Jacob Zuma's re-election as president in 2013, the first publicly open lesbian is named in the cabinet. Lynne Brown is given the job of heading the department of Public Works. A few months later the justice minister Jeffrey Radebe is seen on television announcing his unequivocal support for the campaign against hate crimes. In July 2014, Mandela's widow Graça Machel is the guest speaker at a conference on violence against lesbians.

Running directly alongside this is the less tolerant aspect of South African society. There is the hesitation and the occasional blatant refusal of some police officers to investigate serious accusations made by homosexual victims of violence. There are the occasions when South African representatives to international organisations have abstained when proposals relating to the discrimination of homosexuals have been put to the vote. And then there is the infamous episode that occurs in 1998 at a meeting of the government's cabinet. South African Communist Party (SACP) leaders are also present, in accordance with its alliance with the ruling ANC party. The SACP supported the 'freedom clause' in the constitution, and a significant number of its members are active in the LGBT movement. The meeting discusses the ramifications of the inclusion of the clause in the new constitution and some express considerable dissatisfaction. Dumisani Makhaye, an ANC leader from the KwaZulu Natal province asks another of those present; "Do you remember what we used to do to gays in our military camps?" "We shot them," comes the reply. It is a sickening boast. Makhaye has never set foot in any ANC military camp, but it's a classic example of the aversion many still have to the idea of homosexuality.

In March 2010, the then minister of Culture Lulu Xingwana walks out of an exhibition by the photographer and activist Zanele Muholi. She describes the portrayal of lesbian love as immoral and offensive, and against the notion of 'nation building'. It echoes the objections made more than twenty years previously by the ANC board member Ruth Mompati in her interview with the British magazine *Capital Gay*. In a foreword to the book 'Sex & Politics in South Africa', published in 2005, Mompati distances herself from the notorious interview, writing that she felt ambushed by the leading questions she was asked by her interviewer. "I had no problem with homosexuality because I didn't think it actually existed within our organisation. It seemed to me to be a European problem. I admit I was from the old school. I grew up in a time when you didn't concern yourself with the private lives of others." Mompati writes she "realises that times have changed and that [her] organisation has endorsed the right to be free from discrimination on the grounds of sexual orientation." She describes it as the 'positive outcome' of a debate in which she was a part. Mompati acknowledges the interview itself was a significant moment in the debate on homosexuality, even though she maintains her outspoken remarks should be taken in context, as they did not completely reflect her viewpoint at the time.

Opinions vary as to who the principle players were who helped push through laws that turned South Africa upside down in such a short space of time. Certainly, Mompati's interview and Mbeki's subsequent reaction were significant. But it would do an injustice to the tireless work carried out by many gay activists across the country to suggest that Mbeki's letter was the main catalyst for the inclusion of the clause in the constitution. Mbeki's feelings about homosexuality were similar to those Mompati mentioned in the foreword to her book – what happens in the bedroom should be of no concern to others. However, the significance of the clause is that it awarded equal rights to homosexuals – it was unequivocally no longer something that just happened behind closed doors. It had come out into the open.

The man who interviewed Mompati, Peter Tatchell, seems to want to claim the lion's share of the credit himself. He believes that South Africa's 'pink revolution' hinged on that infamous interview, and as light follows day – on the interviewer. It leaves little space for the crucial role that others played.

There is another school of thought that argues South African homosexuals have to thank the 'special composition of its population' for their freedom. In other words: because there are so many European oriented white people. This rather intriguing analysis holds a curious appeal, mainly due to its comical political incorrectness, but it bears little resemblance to the facts. After all, for decades white South Africans vote overwhelmingly to keep a regime in power that maintains a hardline stance against homosexuals, and which at one point wants to tighten even further the anti-gay laws that are already considered draconian.

What certainly contributes to the speed of legal change in South Africa is the confusion and dismay shown by the members of the white churches that had for so long given their blessing to the politics of apartheid. During the course of the 1980s, doubts grow concerning this collaboration with the white minority regime, and it leads to a paralysis amongst churchgoers and clergy alike. There is a realisation that they are standing still whilst change is happening all around. They can no longer take for granted that they are the sole custodians of morality; after all, the values that underlined orthodox Christian thought are being wholeheartedly undermined. In a flash, homosexuality, as well as abortion, is no longer illegal, and women's rights are being advocated by anyone with an eye on the modern world. And what next? The death penalty is abolished but euthanasia might be legalised. Should we show our contempt for such change? If any resistance is ever contemplated, it never sees the light of day, and secretly, there are many within the church who harbour a certain pride that their country, with a living saint as president, is being praised worldwide for its stance on freedom and human rights. What has been trampled on for so long is now central to South Africa's international image. It's clearly no accident that, of the first ten countries that have legalised gay marriage, so many are former dictatorships: Spain, Portugal, Argentina, and of course South Africa. Just as with homophobia, it can be argued that the expression of its exact opposite should be viewed in the right context. Higher interests are at stake than an absolute conviction of the righteousness of equality. Being pro-gay stands for openness and understanding. In other words, everything that the previous dictatorships were not.

It's now known that homosexual Cape activists in the 1980s, who are just as involved as Simon Nkoli in the fight against apartheid, had already started lobbying various influential ANC members living in exile. Albie Sachs is one. He will later take his place as a judge in the Constitutional Court and is seen as being sympathetic to their cause. But according to the lawyer Kader Asmal, who held a number of different ministerial posts between 1994 and 2004, Sachs at that point in time considered there was little chance of success in including a specific homosexual clause into the new constitution.

Lobbying was certainly influential. Take for example the discussions members of the international solidarity movement conduct with ANC officials, talks that undoubtedly contribute to the eventual willingness of the freedom movement to grant equal rights to gays. Zackie Achmat goes as far to suggest that the 'conversion' of the ANC is almost solely due to the Dutch anti-apartheid movement. In an interview he gives to the magazine *Chimurenga* in May 2003 he says: "There were many *moffies* active in the movement (...), and in meetings with ANC members in exile, they were constantly stressing the importance of including gay rights on the agenda. It certainly helped to change their opinions." But just as with the *Capital Gay* interview, the lobbying from Cape Town and the support from the Netherlands, one mustn't overestimate its significance. The proposals that the likes of Sachs and Asmal make in the 1980s should be seen as a symptom of the new thinking inside the ANC rather than its origin. The key to the success of South Africa's gay movement must be traced back to the fierce debates that took place behind prison walls in the mid-1980s. These are all men striving for the same ideals – a free and democratic South Africa – but who have different sexual preferences. It's because of this simple fact that, eventually, the communal (the fight against apartheid) and the diverse (the fight for sexual freedom) become reconciled, with a realisation that they are not mutually exclusive. In a free land everyone must feel free. This conclusion is in line with the slogan printed on countless t-shirts, pamphlets, banners and badges, and which becomes synonymous with the South African struggle for freedom — 'an injury to one is an injury to all'.

Of even greater importance is the fact that the debate over equal rights is not a 'white' discussion. The talks are not being driven by a privileged few. The call for sexual freedom comes from those that are oppressed, and from those who empathise with their cause. But the end result is for every LGBT South African.

*

It is October 2013. Mogoeng Mogoeng has been at the helm of the Constitutional Court for two years – a moment for the weekly *Mail & Guardian* to take stock. The judgement of the newspaper, which was fiercely opposed to his nomination, is strikingly positive. The Chief Justice has "adapted to his new surroundings well" and has "climbed to the pinnacle of the legal profession with consummate ease", it pronounces. And importantly, "although he has made no secret of his strong religious faith, he is no fanatic". His judgements are "completely in line with the constitution", and he has shown himself to be an "astute interrogator". What has been striking is Mogoeng's unequivocal determination to appoint more female judges, and during interviews has been assiduous in asking candidates about their experiences of sexism. In the first two years of his term, Mogoeng Mogoeng seems to have become won over by a constitution that he has sworn to defend.

Chapter 2

Stoking the fire

Hot on the heels of South Africa's monumental changes, the Zimbabwean president Robert Mugabe comes out of the closet as the commander-in-chief of Africa's anti-gay brigade. The ensuing witch-hunt is locking horns with the forces of change.

The news of South Africa's transitional constitution spreads across the continent like wildfire: a 'freedom clause' has been included that gives equality to LGBT people. It's time for gay activists to spread the word. Internet, e-mails and mobile phones are not widely used in Africa in the early 1990s, but a few campaigners hear of these remarkable developments via their Western contacts from other international gay movements. The new democratic South Africa exerts an almost magical power for people in other African countries. They can only dream of equality and a life free from the risk of persecution. In cities such as Johannesburg and Cape Town, an African LGBT community is growing rapidly. The excitement is contagious. Messages are quickly sent to the 'front'. Tourists, development aid workers, businessmen and conference-goers all play their part, informing friends and acquaintances on the gay scene. Advocates for equal rights are making use of the technological revolution that is slowly but surely taking a hold, whilst gay Africans living abroad use the more traditional methods of phoning and writing to tell their friends back home. *Radio trottoir* does the rest – spreading the message by word of mouth. Newspapers and radio stations, on the other hand, play a marginal role.

This is news that inspires Africans from all walks of life and gives them an incentive to strive for something similar in their own lives. This new transitional constitution in South Africa serves as a wake-up call to the whole continent, and gives a massive shot in the arm to a blossoming gay activism in Africa. But there is a downside too – this burgeoning excitement also stokes the fire of a counter-movement. The race to neutralise the gains is just about to start.

Many of Africa's leaders are following the developments in South Africa with intense interest. For years its troubled history and the politics of apartheid have dominated Pan-African summits. These meetings would invariably end with a strongly worded declaration attacking the white minority government. Pretoria, the home of the apartheid government, is viewed as the main source of division and strife, not only in South Africa itself, but elsewhere on the continent too.

It is accused of being jointly responsible for fomenting civil wars in other countries such as Angola and Mozambique, destabilising the entire region. Neighbouring Namibia has been occupied by South Africa for years. The international community is reluctant to act on Africa's call to increase the pressure on Pretoria, seeing the regime of P.W. Botha — nicknamed the *Great Crcodile* by his supporters — as an important ally in the fight against communism. The Cold War is impeding any genuine development in the southern regions of the continent. Violent and bloody conflicts are being fought which, however localised they may seem, are in reality a struggle for hegemony between East and West, and the control of the continent's vast mineral wealth.

South Africa's neighbours see themselves as 'front-line states'. Many have a large South African exile community and a few allow ANC military camps within their borders. The movement's headquarters are in the Zambian capital Lusaka, and the Zimbabwean capital Harare is often the favoured venue for international conferences against apartheid. In an attempt to stifle this support, Pretoria carries out a number of terrorist attacks in countries it perceives as ANC allies. The aim is to instil a sense of unease and fear in the country's leaders. It works handsomely in Mozambique where, as a result of severe provocation, the government signs a peace agreement with Pretoria in the mid-1980s. Botha's apartheid regime is aiding anti-communist Renamo rebels who are involved in a series of brutal civilian massacres in its attempt to overthrow Mozambique's left-leaning government. In exchange for help from South Africa, the rebels intimidate ANC supporters living in exile, forcing many to flee. However, under the terms of the new peace accord, Pretoria has agreed to stop shoring up the rebels. The Mozambican government keeps to its promise, Pretoria doesn't. Its army continues to give financial and military support to the rebels for many more years.

The Zimbabwean leader Robert Mugabe is seen as the self-appointed commander-in-chief of the 'front-line states' and, *ipso facto,* of the international campaign to isolate the minority government in Pretoria. In 1989, this role ends once F.W. de Klerk succeeds President P.W. Botha, who had suffered a stroke. De Klerk quickly indicates that he is prepared to change tack and shows a willingness to start negotiating with the liberation movement over dismantling the government's racist policies. The slate is wiped clean and the decades-long campaign against Pretoria is finally declared over. But for the likes of Mugabe, the campaign waged against his neighbour has been a useful tool in diverting attention from the problems in his own country, where there is little to cheer about. Furthermore, a new leader has emerged — one who seems prepared to join his former enemies around the negotiating table. Nelson Mandela is the future, a leader advocating a new form of democracy in Africa. One that not only removes apartheid from the political landscape, but the one-party state too – the antithesis of the system enforced by Mugabe and many of his African colleagues. Mandela has chosen a multi-party democracy and, to rub salt into the wound, has declared that he will remain as president, if elected, for one term only. It must feel like a slap in the face to many of the continent's leaders who are competing with each other for who can hold the reins of power the longest. There seems to be little warmth between Mandela and Mugabe, especially as the latter has made no secret of wanting to cling to office until his death. Mandela is true to his word and in 1999 retreats from public office, after one term as president. He describes the 'failing leadership' of the Zimbabwean president as 'tragic'. Mugabe responds by calling Mandela 'a puppet of the West'.

In the first few years after Mandela's release, there is a gradual realisation for many of Africa's leaders that this glorious South African spring – the result of a collective struggle against apartheid – is likely to threaten their own survival just as much as South African extremists who'd pressed for the continuation of white rule.

Of course, it is important to show the outside world a united front. After all, they had been calling for the abolition of apartheid with endless regularity. In May 1994, most of Africa's leaders attend Mandela's inauguration as South Africa's first democratically elected president. But when former prisoner 466/64 calls for a respect for universal human rights and rejects the principle of 'African solidarity', one can almost hear an audible collective grumble of discontent. This is a thinly disguised criticism of a form of rule that unanimously condemns all evil perpetrated outside the continent, whilst simultaneously brushing aside every evil committed from within. Many African leaders take the view that the Western trait of failing to admonish its own human rights violations is hypocritical. After all, Western leaders are only too prompt to condemn others when they overstep the mark. Some consider human rights to be a 'Western concept', and at odds with African norms and values. The Western principle protects the rights of the individual whilst African traditionalists emphasise the importance of the collective interest – a viewpoint that is now gaining ground in South Africa.

At a seminar discussing homosexuality at the Institute for Contextual Theology in the mid-1990s, the lawyer Edwin Cameron is asked for his reaction to the conspicuous silence of the eighty church leaders also present. "Do they have a problem with the 'freedom clause' in the constitution?" is the question. "If that's true, then please let your concerns be known," is Cameron's response. "As long as we carry on as though we're all in agreement, we're not going to get anywhere." It works. One of the church leaders responds and explains that they certainly respect the constitution, but consider it to be a 'product of the West'. The negotiations were a matter of give and take, he explains, in order not to make the whites, who were being forced to cede power, seem too impotent. The Western influence in the constitution was an olive branch to smooth the path to democracy. This remark angers Barney Pityana, the chair of the South African Human Rights Commission, who is also present: "If our constitution, with its respect for human rights, is a Western construct, then torture must be African," he exclaims. This incendiary remark kills the discussion stone dead. What does the church leader mean? Is he supportive of torture? Obviously not. But one can only guess what he's implying. Does he consider the likening of gay rights to human rights as contravening African values? If so, the man has failed to remember that the South African constitution was written and devised without any appreciable Western interference. It is self-evident that legal experts involved in the process would have been aware of examples elsewhere in the world, and would have used them as a loose template, but the final deliberations and content are one hundred per cent South African.

The same cannot be said of Zimbabwe. The Lancaster House Accord of 1980 contains very clear traces of British interference. The irony, in this instance, is that it did not culminate in an end to the anti-gay laws introduced during the British colonial period. It's a classic example of the postcolonial paradox: the anti-gay rhetoric evokes a yearning for 'African values' and a distaste for Western aberrations – but there are situations where leaders such as Mugabe are only too happy to cling on to laws dating back to the Victorian era. In his 2011 autobiography, Morgan Tsvangirai, Zimbabwe's first opposition leader as the head of the Movement for Democratic Change, makes light of Mugabe's claim to be a socialist or a tribalist. "He makes me think of a British Lord," he writes.

'What is Mandela's fascination with the West?' many African leaders were asking each other. The South African president, in his first years in office, is attempting to keep his multitude of fans across the world happy by embarking on a series of official visits. He travels frequently to Europe, Asia and the US, whilst other African rulers are forced to stay closer to home to deal with campaigns aimed at ending their political dominance and preventing them from enjoying a third, fourth, even a fifth term in office – the call for constitutional reform growing ever louder in an increasing number of countries. Some leaders sneer at Mandela's attempts in 1995 to prevent the execution of the Nigerian writer and activist Ken Saro Wiwa. Why is he meddling in things that don't concern him? Don't African countries respect each other's sovereignty anymore? If Sani Abacha, the Nigerian dictator at the time, wants to hang the controversial writer, then surely that's an 'internal matter' and no-one has any right to contradict it. Or so the reasoning goes.

Meanwhile, a number of international development organisations close their headquarters in Harare and Lusaka and move to Johannesburg. International conferences also migrate southwards. It seems the liberation of South Africa is coming at a significant material cost to its neighbours. Conversely, South African multi-nationals are exploring the possibilities elsewhere on the continent. The market has suddenly opened up after years of boycott, and these companies, still predominantly run by whites, grasp the new opportunities with both hands. This also sets the blood boiling, and is quickly condemned as a new form of imperialism. 'South Africa is behaving just like the United States,' is being whispered behind the scenes at meetings of the Pan-African family.

The antipathy that some African leaders feel for the ANC, and Mandela in particular, has deep historical roots. Despite the black-nationalist aspirations of most African independence movements, the ANC adopts a 'non-racial politics' in 1965. Races are a fantasy and one should not think in colours. This non-racial principle becomes part of the mainstream ideology of the movement. The Freedom Charter contains a key sentence: "South Africa belongs to everyone who lives there, black and white". Its inclusion is fiercely debated within the ANC, but it concludes that it's fighting a system and not the specific population responsible for introducing it. This is a bridge too far for some African leaders.

The alliance the ANC makes with the South African Communist Party is another case in point. The then Libyan leader Colonel Gaddafi describes the ANC as an "accomplice to Zionist Israel". The fact that one of the most prominent ANC leaders is Joe Slovo, a Jew and a Communist, is seen as incontrovertible evidence. According to the former president Thabo Mabeki, Gaddafi gave the ANC no financial or military support in its fight against apartheid. That Mugabe and the ANC worked closely together also belongs to the realm of fiction. Mugabe's sympathies during the apartheid years lay more with the PAC (Pan Africanist Congress), a small splinter group that goes its own way after the ANC adopts its non-racial charter. Mugabe's relationship with China in this period is also close, the latter being no friend of Moscow during the Cold War.

And then insult is added to injury: equal rights for homosexuals is enshrined into the South African constitution. Many African leaders see it as proof of the continued white dominance in the country, even though these are the same whites that for decades have supported the anti-gay laws of the apartheid regime. Just as the democratic changes are beginning to undermine the authority of Africa's many potentates, gay activists across the continent see something to give them hope and inspiration. In Zimbabwe, members of GALZ (Gays and Lesbians of Zimbabwe), a small and predominantly white organisation, pluck up the courage to register their own stall at the Harare International Book Fair. They intend to present a book containing the stories of Zimbabwean gays and lesbians. The aim is to draw attention to something that many of the population believe doesn't exist in Africa. To say that its objective falls flat would be an understatement. Most Africans prefer to close their eyes to homosexuality – it isn't part of their culture, tradition or religion. A book like this is contrary to the normal practice of keeping quiet – a collective 'don't ask, don't tell' policy. But the new South African constitution has changed all that. A new 'freedom clause' has specifically mentioned LGBT people, and given them equal rights. The right to be free from discrimination on the grounds of sexual orientation makes a direct reference to the fact that more than just one preference exists. The door has been pushed wide open and gay activists see the chance to seize the initiative. They want to be called gay and lesbian and take part in pride parades. Gay bars and cafes must open, and lesbian football teams must be established. LGBT organisations must be set up, for transgender and bisexual people too. But there is a limit to their candour — the new groups choose obscure titles such as the 'Gentleman's Alliance of Livelihood International'. It's a throwback to a post-war Europe when gay organisations, in the Netherlands for example, are given names such as the 'Shakespeare Club', the forerunner of the COC (*Centrum voor Ontspanning en Cultuur* – the Centre for Relaxation and Culture). Activists are increasingly using frames of reference that many Africans have never even heard of. That women go with other women, they are well aware, and everyone has an uncle or a nephew who flouts convention and who doesn't go with women. But gay? Lesbian? LGBT? Gay rights? Gay movements? This is something completely new.

The book fair is the biggest in Africa, with publishers from 120 countries taking part. Under pressure from the Zimbabwean authorities, a stall for GALZ is refused. It causes a scandal: four board members of the book fair quit, and countless writers sign a petition calling for GALZ's participation. All to no avail. There is to be no last minute change of heart. President Mugabe is present at the opening and uses his speech to make an unprecedented attack on gays and lesbians. He's surrounded by members of his cabinet and, according to witnesses, they almost 'wet their pants laughing' as their leader proceeds to ridicule GALZ. Amongst those witnessing the spectacle are two Nobel laureates, the Nigerian Wole Soyinka and the South African Nadine Gordimer, both of whom have signed the petition. They're deeply shocked by what they hear. The speech is broadcast live on Zimbabwean television, the normal practice whenever Mugabe speaks in public. The speech is now often cited as an example of homophobia of the highest order, and with good reason. Mugabe makes it abundantly clear that gays and lesbians have no entitlement to any rights whatsoever, and describes GALZ as "an organisation of sodomites and perverts". He justifies his remarks with a reference to the 'worldwide known' maxim: sex is not performed in public. "Of course, sex is permitted within marriage, that goes without saying (...) but no-one has the right to do it wherever they wish." These are the rules, Mugabe declares, "because the intimate nature of sex demands privacy". He then states that it's only logical that an organisation that espouses 'sex in public' has no right to promote and present books on the subject. So, according to Mugabe, it's not about homosexuality *per se,* but the messianic zeal with which they attempt to set up their own stall and endorse a book. GALZ wants to let the world know of its existence and be part of a movement that advocates gay rights. For Mugabe, it is abundantly clear – this equates to 'sex in public'.

Mugabe's speech causes a sensation. There is astonishment, as well as support, but its context is quickly lost. GALZ was never forced to close its doors. This suggests that the authorities turn a blind eye to such things as long as one doesn't flaunt one's position. Mugabe knows only too well there are many homosexuals living in Zimbabwe; after all, he has one of the best secret services on the continent at his disposal. There is also the case of his predecessor. Canaan Banana was a Methodist priest and the first president of the newly independent Zimbabwe. He was also gay. Although married, it was later exposed as a sham in a book his wife wrote about their relationship published shortly after she sought political asylum in London. Rumours over Banana's affairs with young men had been circulating for decades. There were claims that the selection of players for the national football team, that he founded, was made purely on the basis of whether they had 'been of service to the president'. Two years after Mugabe's tirade at the Harare book fair, Banana is found guilty of sexual abuse. He denies the accusations, describing homosexuality as 'deviant, abominable and wrong', but flees to South Africa whilst on bail. It takes Nelson Mandela to convince him that justice should run its course, and so Banana returns to Zimbabwe and is promptly sentenced to eleven years in prison, of which nine are suspended. He serves just a short time before being released in 2001, dying of cancer two years later.

Two weeks after the opening of the book fair Mugabe, makes another homophobic speech. The occasion is the annual Independence Day celebrations, and this time he ratchets up the rhetoric even further by calling for arrests to be made. The behaviour of gays and lesbians is, he says, "worse than pigs and dogs". In 2010 he apologises for having made the remarks: "I didn't realise then how much I had offended dogs with those comments."

There has been much speculation on the underlying causes of Mugabe's diatribes. It's unlikely to have been the result of a well thought out strategy. But he certainly needs something to divert attention from other troubling issues in Zimbabwe. There is considerable disquiet over the economic downturn in the country. His government is being criticised by its own party members for being too tightly controlled by the IMF and the World Bank. In the 1980s, Zimbabwe, as with many other African countries, is tied to a strict 'structural adjustment programme' imposed by the two main international lending bodies. It's forced to make dramatic cuts to its spending programme, with education and the health services being severely affected. This goes hand in hand with a significant increase in corruption. The veterans of the independence struggle feel betrayed by rulers who are feathering their own nests, but failing to protect their former comrades in arms from the economic fallout.

Mugabe's speech at the book fair is most probably not deliberately designed to unleash a witch-hunt against gays and lesbians. The intention is more likely to force GALZ, and all Zimbabwean homosexuals, to shut the closet door firmly behind them. But the strong feelings the speech arouse may well spark in Mugabe's mind an idea that, by encouraging a hate campaign, he'll be able to kill two birds with one stone. The veterans will turn their anger on others and not him, and he can once again point an accusing finger at the former colonial masters by suggesting that the actions of GALZ has the fingerprints of the West all over it. South Africa's neo-colonial tyranny can also be targeted, and Mandela in particular, with his gay friendly constitution. Another factor that must not be overlooked is Mugabe's grim experiences during the darkest days of the fight for independence, and how it affects his subsequent judgements as leader. In order to sow division between the black freedom movements, the ruling white minority government of Ian Smith had attempted to vilify Mugabe by distributing disparaging pamphlets about him. He is, for example, accused of being homosexual. There is no doubt that Mugabe's aversion to homosexuality is partly due to this smear campaign, but his experiences in prison may also have played their part. The Zimbabwean psychologist Lynde Francis, who befriends Mugabe in the 1980s, is convinced that the tone and body language of his televised diatribes point to experiences of sexual abuse. Still, the question remains whether existing homophobic resentments would have risen to the surface if political expediency hadn't been an issue. The underlying motives of GALZ must also be questioned. There is more at stake than just an appeal for equal rights for one section of Zimbabwean society. The South African academic Peter Vale believes that the activism surrounding the Harare book fair is a precursor of the emerging democratic shifts taking place in many African countries. "The gay activists are breaking down the culture of deference to the leader. They dare to contradict him. That was unheard of. That was, until then, completely unthinkable."

The realisation that gay activism is stoking the flames of unrest and injecting an urgency into the fight *for* democracy and *against* corruption causes other African leaders to take stock. Taking inspiration from Mugabe's diatribes, and looking for ways to deflect criticism from the growing discontent concerning corruption, poverty and abuse of power, they begin to include homophobia into their speeches with outrageous aplomb. Mugabe has blamed a severe drought in his country on gays. His political counterparts in Cameroon follow it up with claims that its economic woes can be traced back to homosexual depravity. In 2014, church leaders in Liberia attribute an outbreak of Ebola to gays; conservative church leaders in the US have already declared that the epidemic is God's punishment and is a warning for people to follow the true path or suffer the consequences. The Namibian leader Sam Nujomo is quick to imitate Mugabe's homophobic rants. During a Women's Congress of his ruling SWAPO party, two transvestites are observed in the ladies' toilets during the break. It's all the excuse the president needs to vent his anger in an indignant tirade.

And so in the second half of the 1990s, the simmering homophobia gathers pace, and spreads from country to country. The public debate is stoked by jittery leaders looking for a scapegoat, leaving many gay activists fearing for their lives. It's a sad dampener to the festivities triggered by South Africa's liberation, and shows how deep-seated the prejudices and misconceptions are. It's clear that the relative ease with which South Africa's liberal constitution is established will not be reproduced in other countries without a struggle. The catalyst for the first hate campaigns in Kenya and Uganda is the news that the first homosexual marriages are taking place in Europe and Latin America. And when a number of 'symbolic' marriages take place in their own countries, it is grist to the mill for those eager to stir up trouble, especially when one of the ceremonies involves a European – more evidence that it's a 'Western import'. In the late 1990s, the Ugandan president Yoweri Museveni calls for homosexuals to be arrested. The country's secret service immediately goes into action. Five gay activists, who work together on a newsletter, are taken to 'safe-houses' – the euphemism used for an interrogation and torture centre run by the Ugandan police. There are moments when corruption can be a useful tool in the on-going struggle for human rights: the activists know that money talks, and are able to buy themselves out of their predicament. Most of them flee to neighbouring Kenya, not the safe haven they would have wished for, but at least they're out of the direct clutches of the Ugandan authorities.

In Zambia, a newspaper interview given by one of the country's first gay activists is the prelude to an intense homophobic media reaction. Emboldened by the encouraging signs of progress elsewhere, the young man agrees to an interview. It's time for homosexuals to reveal themselves and start to openly question the widely held prejudices that pervade Zambian life, he says. The country has officially been declared a Christian nation in 1991, and many Zambians simply refuse to believe that homosexuals exist there. For this reason, the young gay man declares that he has already slept with twenty-four other men. More convincing proof that there are living, breathing homosexuals in Zambia would be harder to find. It causes a furore. The newspaper is inundated with letters from outraged readers, and the organisation the young man has helped found must immediately forget any thoughts of becoming officially registered. His friends no longer greet him in the street for fear of being associated with him, and branded gay. Not long after the interview, Zambia's first gay whistle-blower flees to South Africa.

Church leaders in Nigeria, President Yahya Jammeh of Gambia, the Egyptian authorities – in the 1990s, they all take turns to express their revulsion of this evil that has dared to rear its head. Even if no threat exists, one can rely upon an angry mob to rail against the 'pink peril'. At the beginning of this century, in the port of Dar es Salaam, the capital of Tanzania, word gets out that a cruise ship full of homosexual tourists is about to descend upon the city. Thousands of Muslims gather to protest. But the sexuality of the tourists is just part of the reason for the anger. These are American tourists, and the US has just begun its invasion of Iraq. Reason enough to set the blood boiling in a country whose population is half Muslim. Journalists from *Behind the Mask*, the internet news site reporting on issues relating to homosexuality across Africa, follow the events with interest, and separate fact from the fiction. They discover that not one American tour operator offers cruises with a stop-over in Tanzania. Clearly, the inherent homophobia is a convenient channel to express equally strident anti-American sentiments.

But it works both ways. Activists from the West have also set the alarm bells ringing on the flimsiest of information. A classic example is the belief that in the Muslim controlled part of northern Nigeria, the death sentence has been handed down to a number of homosexuals on the basis of Islamic Sharia law – a sentence that is carried out by stoning. But where is the proof? It's only in 2014 that the first gay couple is arrested – and then released. Sharia law states there has to be at least four witnesses to the act. In this instance, the necessary evidence is not forthcoming and the couple are freed. One of the problems facing international human rights organisations in confirming the veracity of a story is that pictures of previous atrocities are often re-used on the internet and ascribed to alleged new incidents elsewhere.

The anti-gay campaigns that spring up in the 1990s are often described as an *offensive*, carried out by politicians, church leaders and tribal chiefs. But it can also be seen as a *defensive* reaction to a movement that is gradually gaining ground, and to an increase in the visibility of gays and lesbians across the continent. African leaders are inciting homophobia, fully conscious that introducing a 'gay friendly' political agenda will have far wider consequences than just the recognition of equal rights for a small minority. Pioneering African LGBT activists, just as feminist women's groups, idiosyncratic artists or outspoken investigative journalists, all threaten the carefully constructed postcolonial framework – a system based on hierarchical and patriarchal norms and values. The 1960s is a decade of dramatic change in Africa, and the leaders of this new social order galvanise their citizens into a collective nation building. The objective is to erase the memories of the ethnic divisions caused by decades of colonial rule. The new rulers want to end, once and for all, the fragmentation of a society in which millions are forced to work far from home, and others driven into exile. Tens of thousands sacrificed their studies, a relationship, or a family for a life in the jungle where the rebel bases fighting for independence were often located. At the same time, and out of necessity, hundreds of thousands co-operated with their colonial rulers. How could all these wounds be healed? From the 1950s onwards, 'Unity, unity, unity' is the cry heard across the continent, from the Ghanaian capital Accra, where it all begins in 1955, to Lesotho's capital Maseru where independence is celebrated a little over ten years later. In the end, it all comes down to one postcolonial dream: no more division.

Society, people, family, Africa. It's no longer necessary for Africans to define themselves on the basis of their tribe, as their colonial masters had done. Kikuyus are now Kenyan, Yorubas are Nigerian, Bembas are Zambian. In contrast to the divide and rule tactics of the former Western rulers, it is now one party, formed from the liberation movement, that dominates. Newspapers are no longer the mouthpiece of colonial propaganda, but are now expected to lead the way in building trust in the new nation-building process.

However, despite so much change, there is much that stays the same. The new rulers follow the lead of their predecessors by embracing a rigid patriarchal power structure. An obedience to the male sex is thought to be the most expedient way to mend a bruised society. Everyone must know their place. But whilst *political* power is now in the hands of Africans, *economic* power is proving more difficult, with control still firmly in the hands of the white elites and the multinationals. The new leaders may well pay lip service to the principles of non-allegiance and the sovereign state, but the reality is that these newly independent countries are still caught in the crossfire between East and West with the continuing Cold War. The inflammatory speeches the black leaders make to packed stadiums, and during meetings with international organisations, are mostly just hot air. In practice, frustrations are building up over a feeling of impotence, as they become increasingly dependent on Western aid and hindered by the accompanying conditions. With little political opposition or pluralism, many of the new generation of leaders begin a realm of self-aggrandisement and a concentration of powers. The process of enrichment and nepotism has taken hold.

Chapter 3

You say yes, I say no

A ritual dance to the same tune. With an unwillingness to compromise and little enthusiasm to see the opposing view, the warring parties are each claiming the upper hand by using 'facts', anthropological discoveries, interpretations of religious texts and assumptions based on characteristics of 'the' African culture.

The message that pastor Tsietsi Thandekiso is going to spread this Sunday morning couldn't be any clearer: there's not one single passage in the Bible that condemns homosexuality. Nowhere! Thandekiso flicks through the book without looking down, as though he's able to sweep away any contentious passage with the touch of his fingers. And he will make his point even more strongly to the assembled congregation — if there's one thing in the scriptures that is unmistakeable and irrefutable, it is this: God cherishes all his creatures without exception. Hallelujah! Praise the Lord! Leviticus 18:22 (you shall not lie with a man as with a woman; it is an abomination) is brushed aside. Another hymn is sung. The setting is a half-filled, improvised church in the former ballroom of the somewhat down-at-heel Harrison Reef Hotel in Hillbrow in the centre of Johannesburg. This is the Hope and Unity Metropolitan Christian Church, and at the end of the 1990s it has become a haven for young gays and lesbians.

At the same time, an international conference of gay activists is taking place in the city. One of the questions being asked is how God's word can be interpreted. Gay theologians are doing their best to read into the Bible what, according to others, doesn't exist; or to suggest meanings that help to serve the gay activists' agenda. It's an exchange of ideas between like-minded people. But then one of the participants, a theologian from Cape Town, poses a question: "Why is everyone present doing their best to counter senseless accusations?" There is silence. "Aren't we just being reactionary?" he continues, a little despairingly. "There's so much in the Bible. Why are we beating ourselves up about it so much?" The chairman of the meeting moves swiftly on to another subject: "We're regularly being told that homosexuality is alien to African traditions and our culture. Is that really the case?" The theologian groans. You can see him thinking: here we go again.

When cataloguing the on-going debate over the rights and wrongs of homosexuality that affects so many

African countries, it is worth using another example to shed light on why it continues to be so contentious: the ritual dances of the Zulus in South Africa, the Masai in Kenya or the Bushmen of the Kalahari, who can all be seen at well-known tourist attractions, performing in traditional costume. It goes as follows: intimidating looking warriors enter the stage; soon, they're confronted by bellicose adversaries; both parties declare war on each other in cries that are unintelligible to Western ears; a guide explains that they're fighting over a girl or a cow; the sheer tenacity in their fighting shows they mean business; finally, the winner is rewarded with the spoils. These are carefully rehearsed acts that include elements from past cultures, and which are occasionally still observed, but give an overall impression that time is standing still. These ostentatious scenes continue to breathe life into the idea that the 'noble savage', a relic from the past, is alive and kicking. The visitor is transported to a terrifying but still believable reality. Africa! And for a large tip the actors are only too happy to cultivate this image.

In the struggle for LGBT rights, the opposing standpoints are as intransigent as the conventions surrounding the African tourist industry. 'Gays do not exist in Africa' was often heard in the 1990s, even, unbelievably, in the direct company of African homosexuals themselves, who would respond with a resounding sigh of disbelief and a collective 'oh yes it does'. 'Oh no it doesn't,' was often the reply. Any argument to the contrary just falls on deaf ears. Opponents sometimes admit there are some Africans who claim to be homosexual, but will adamantly declare that these have become infected with a Western disease. After all, over the course of hundreds of years, explorers and plunderers on the African coastline passed on a variety of sexual diseases not seen on the continent before, they claim. It's also argued that anything that deviates from the accepted norm of heterosexuality is contrary to authentic African culture and tradition. In this state of affairs there exists just one unmistakeable culture from which all unequivocal, modern day traditions have arisen. There's no room for homosexuality in this interpretation. It's a hypothesis, according to LGBT activists, that is easily contradicted by the bookshelves full of anthropological studies that indicate a veritable wonderland of same-sex *joie de vivre* in former times.

Here are a handful of examples. In previous centuries, the Mossi Kings in Burkina Faso had relationships with their pages who would adorn themselves in women's attire for special occasions. In the former Kingdom of Dahomey in modern day Benin, marriage between women, the Dahomey Amazons, was nothing unusual. The Zulu King Shaka encouraged non-penetrative sex between his soldiers as a prelude to battle. Amongst the Azande in the former Zaire, so-called 'boy-wives' were an accepted part of society. Documents from a Dutch military attaché, who lived in the Ndongo Kingdom in Angola in the late 1740s, reveal the story of Nzinga, a warrior woman who dressed in men's clothes and who surrounded herself with a harem of men dressed in women's clothes. Other cross-dressers are chronicled by the anthropologist Jean-Baptiste Labat in his travels through the Congo in the eighteenth century. The traditional laws of the

Shona in Zimbabwe recognize the existence of relationships between men. Rock drawings in Zimbabwe, that are thousands of years old, show males in a clear state of arousal — and not a single woman in sight. According to a flyer attributed to an LGBT association in Johannesburg, such representations can also be seen in drawings of the San – the former Bushmen of South Africa. How many drawings? 'At least one,' according to a rather hopeful anthropological study. The Igbo (Nigeria), the Nuer (Sudan), the Kuria (Tanzania), the Cape Bantu (South Africa), the Kisii (Kenya) and the Baganda in Uganda all include men who behave as women and women who behave as men, from the highest ranks to the lowest order.

Some etymologists also suggest that some of the original languages spoken on the continent include words for homosexual, such as *hungonchani* in Shona and *bukhontxana*, a word used by Mozambican mineworkers in South Africa to describe marriages that are known to have taken place in these circles. Another example is the Zulu word *setabane*, although linguists emphasize the negative connotation of the term. One might also add the Afrikaner word *agtermekaarkêrel* (behind each other male).

What is striking is that each side, in an attempt to gain the upper hand, is inclined to use examples from pre-colonial Africa to clarify and further enhance their positions. Opponents dream of an Africa of heterosexual harmony, with a distinct sense of community and a clear division of roles between a man and a woman – the latter naturally holding the subordinate position. Supporters talk of an African history awash with diversity and sexual freedom. Both sides seem to agree that their perfect world was destroyed by foreign rulers. The untold damage that Western and Arab slave-traders have done to the continent can only be guessed at, and the same, of course, goes for the rule of the colonial powers. But according to the South African Muslim theologian Farid Esack "not all foreign influence has been bad." As a fervent advocate of a progressive Islam for many years, he emphasizes: "The workers' union is a Western idea, and protests against slavery also started in the West."

The Cameroonian academic Basile Ndjio has published numerous papers relating to homophobia in his country, but remains unimpressed with the anthropological conclusions made thus far and which have been used to strengthen the arguments of the pro lobby. When questioned on his research, he observes dryly, "Just because it existed in the Africa of old, doesn't mean that it's normal." It doesn't help that the majority of the studies examining homosexuality in Africa is being carried out by white, Western researchers. Critics insinuate that these researchers are hunting for proof of something they already consider to be unquestionably true. But aren't the examples given indisputable proof? Certainly not, the critics respond. A woman who marries another woman is not a lesbian. How could you possibly think that? And what about the rock drawings of the men who are clearly excited to be with each other? 'One will always see things that one wants to see,' is the reply, usually accompanied with a wry smile.

And so it goes, round and round. It's a conversation between the deaf, in which both sides are so set in their ways that they're not able to see the wood for the trees. With hand on heart, someone can earnestly declare that they have never come across a homosexual in Africa, and will then accuse every black gay of actually being white. The LGBT activist, on the other hand, may well declare, looking at you straight in the eye, that homosexuality originated in Africa. And it's not long before Queen Victoria gets a mention. Before her reign, before slavery and colonialism, everything was rosy in Africa's garden. It were the whites who introduced homophobia to the continent, especially the British whites, with their nineteenth century legislation that were particularly preoccupied with curbing love between men. The questionable opinion that love between women was spared the lawman's intrusive eye is said to be because Queen Victoria believed such a thing impossible. LGBT activists might have a point concerning the historical accuracy of the Victorians' homophobia, but opponents can also use it to their own advantage. The colonial occupiers, in their considerable ignorance, regarded blacks as primitive and savage, and thus assumed, with little thought behind it, that the 'dark continent' was one big cesspit of perversions and abnormalities, and must be quickly brought to heel. And so the argument goes, with opponents conjuring up all sorts of fantasies to fit snugly into their view of the world.

The word 'savage' evokes images of fierce wild animals, untamed and impossible to control. It has been an expedient analogy for those wishing to vilify homosexuality. In the view of the Zimbabwean president Robert Mugabe, homosexuals should take a good look at the animal kingdom for inspiration. After all, their behaviour is 'worse than dogs and pigs'. The president is apparently no fan of the latter, but their behaviour is certainly better than that of gays. His Gambian counterpart Yahya Jammeh, who seized power in a military coup in 1994, is in agreement. His conviction is based on his long-term study of the behaviour of chickens and turkeys. "I have never seen any evidence of homosexual behaviour in these animals," he says. His expertise extends to the field of AIDS, where he claims that it can be cured with the help of a herb massage and bananas. The former president of Nigeria, General Olusegun Obasanjo, is on record as saying that homosexuality is an abomination, on a par with bestiality, predominantly 'sex with horses'. In a panel discussion in 2010, in which such luminaries as the former British prime minister Tony Blair, the former Secretary General of the United Nations Kofi Annan, the musician Bob Geldof and the human rights defender Graça Machel, are all taking part, it is put to Obasanjo that politicians should not interfere with what happens behind closed doors in the bedroom. It is a private matter. "Privacy?" the Nigerian reacted with shock, "Sex with a horse in your bedroom does not fall under the right to privacy." Kofi Annan, an ardent supporter of equal rights, sighs, and at the end of the debate is heard to say: "I'll work on him." And while he's at it, Annan might consider a visit to see Uganda's first lady Janet Museveni. In March 2014, she entertains her audience with the assertion that she has never heard of there ever being such a thing as a gay cow. There is cheering, but no mooing.

On the subject of animals, there is another line of reasoning used by opponents of homosexuality. Take Umar Inuwa Obi for example, a thirty-two year old student in Bauchi, a town in northern Nigeria. In an interview on Nigerian television he says, "God doesn't tolerate homosexuals; we are not animals." His fellow countryman Uchenna Ocheoha agrees. In February 2014, he writes an article on a Christian website that states, "Gays often use examples from the animal kingdom in an attempt to bring credence to their own behaviour, but even if an animal is doing it, it's still not normal." So much for your gay rights activists' extensive list of pink animal practices! The website *GayUganda* contains a whole gallery of them: the legendary 'pink' penguins, sheep, albatrosses, and even cockroaches. And that is exactly what they are, cockroaches, according to the former Ugandan Minister for Ethics, James Nsaba Buturo. When discussing the topic, he adds that "these are animals that don't participate in anal sex." The Ghanaian politician Joseph Yamin, in searching for a suitable response to the liberal views on homosexuality being shown by the new Gender Minister Nana Oye Lithur, says that he is in agreement with her: gays *do* deserve certain rights — because 'animals also have rights'.

But Africa is not the only part of the world that has invoked the use of the animal kingdom in its discourse on homosexuality. The United States can also be a master of the invective. In October 2010, a number of exotic animals escaped from a zoo in Zanesville, Ohio, at the same time as the campaign was heating up to nominate the Republican candidate for the presidency. The Evangelist Pat Robertson, who had thrown his name into the hat two decades before (with little success) and was now giving it another go, declares that the animals have escaped "with God's help, in order that they can go and bite the gays". It's a statement endorsed by other politicians in the state. The extreme right-wing Republican Michele Bachman, however, distances herself from the remarks, but proposes that the animals should be expelled from the country and shipped back to the Congo. So we are, once more, conveniently back in Africa.

And it is here that a number of anti-gay crusaders have been showing themselves as fervently 'anally obsessed'. A classic example is the documentary series made by the British author and actor Stephen Fry in 2013. Fry can be seen in conversation with a Ugandan pastor. As the interview progresses it becomes increasingly animated, with the pastor repeatedly returning to the issue of anal sex, despite Fry's attempts to change the subject. The actor is visibly shocked and says he does not understand what his interviewee is talking about. "I'm not interested in it, I've never done it and that goes for most of my gay friends too," he says in a defensive but irritated tone. The pastor is unconvinced. His "obsession with sodomy", as Fry describes it, has, of course, everything to do with a revulsion of specific 'deviant' sexual acts (especially when it involves men), and is certainly not a uniquely African obsession. Lesbian sex, on the other hand, which is often used in heterosexual porn films, gets an easier ride, with the proviso that it is for the enjoyment of the male consumer. Furthermore, as supporters for equal rights are at pains to stress, anal sex is by no means the exclusive domain of gay men. A few years ago, the Ghanaian doctor Earnest Yorke articulated another fear relating to anal sex: it leads to a weakening sphincter. It is a logical line of thought, but one that becomes far less believable when accompanied by Yorke's conclusion that this is the reason for so many gay men wearing tights!

There is another factor that must be added to the equation. It is not specific to Africa per se, but certainly to all developing countries: the importance of offspring. Where state pensions and other social safety nets are non-existent or inadequate, there is often a great stress on the need to have many children. They can look after you if you're no longer able to, and because in some parts of the continent the child mortality rate is still significantly high, it's best to play safe and have as many as possible. Although it's perfectly feasible for gays and lesbians to have children themselves, an anxiety still permeates African society that the necessary provisions for old age are being undermined. It is nothing unusual for Africans to tolerate the exploration of one's homosexual feelings, as long as it runs in tandem with a heterosexual relationship and the begetting of children.

Demographics is also playing an increasingly influential role, with a belief that the larger the population, the better. According to the American academic and blogger Scott Long, there now exists, especially in the US and Russia, influential extreme right-wing lobby groups who are tapping into nationalistic aspirations for a greater representation of the 'indigenous' population. In Long's view, this 'demographic argument' is likely to become more of an issue than homosexuality whether moral, religious or cultural. For this reason, in the eyes of someone like the Russian president Vladimir Putin, homosexuality is dangerous because it is a direct challenge to the desire for a continuing population growth. 'Gay propaganda' is prohibited specifically with the intention of preserving the legitimacy of 'right-minded Russians'. His American equivalents – the right-wing Christian movements – see a demographic superiority as a buffer against what they perceive as an advancing Islam. For some African leaders, the concept of national purification – the creation of a nation untainted by any foreign contamination – is a worthy goal, and stems from a deep seated paranoia of everything the West believes in. This is something that always comes at a cost to human lives, or so the perception goes. The name Angola means 'empty land', a painful reminder of millions of transported slaves. In the colonial German South-West Africa, now known as Namibia, the army experimented with genocide on the country's Herero people. The British, Portuguese and Belgian colonial rulers were also culpable in numerous massacres. Explorers travelling through Africa spread sexual diseases. The generation to generation re-telling of these ignominious events has created a breeding ground for distrust and suspicion. It's not helped by some Africans' assertion that the HIV virus was developed in a laboratory in Switzerland with the specific intention of decimating Africa's population. Historical traumas tend to further intensify the zealous embracing of intra-connecting relationships within communities and families that had been torn apart by centuries of disruption. The ramshackle way in which some postcolonial states function serves to reinforce the desire for order and structure even further. It is for this reason that supposedly strong, patriarchal ideologies hold such a powerful allure. Anyone who is persistently antagonistic will be lucky to live to tell the tale.

The South African philosopher and commentator Eusebius McKaiser says that many gay people have allowed themselves to be lured into following the line of discourse drawn up by their opponents. As a consequence, some gay couples are declaring their behaviour so exemplary that heterosexuals could do worse than to follow in their footsteps. Children adopted by gays couldn't be happier, and if gays were in charge in Rwanda in the first few years of the 1990s, without question the genocide against Tutsis and moderate Hutus would never have taken place. To further prove their point, gay activists in Uganda had the idea of launching a cleaning initiative to 'save' the Nile. Avocado plantations would also be installed along the banks of the river. The announcement of their involvement would only have been made once the actions had been deemed successful. It seemed to them to be a fitting rebuke to the incessant accusations that they are the cause of so many of the continent's natural disasters.

Chapter 4

Is Africa different or just the same?

About lesbian men, gents and ladies. Fantasies run wild regarding the specifics of an African sexual identity. But do they do it so differently there?

He walks with a firm and rather nonchalant swagger, his hat pulled down over his eyes. His dark blue trousers are a size too big and hang loosely on his legs. His shirt has been tucked in without much care. When he wolf-whistles at the girls on the other side of the street, they all turn around and look at him. He looks pleased with himself and continues walking. It's the end of the nineties and we're in Katutura, the township close to Windhoek, the capital of Namibia. And here we find Soften, a *lesbian man*.

His girlfriends sometimes have difficulty with his promiscuous behaviour. Soften sees it differently. Biologically he's female, but he considers himself to be a man, one hundred percent. "I love girls in dresses. It's okay if they sometimes wear trousers, but not too often," he says, with a frown on his face. Soften is a member of the Rainbow Warriors, a football team made up only of lesbian men and a single *lady*. A *lady* is the name he gives to a woman he flirts with, charms and makes a pass at. For Soften, every conquest confirms his manliness. It sounds like a very traditional type of man. "Yes," he nods proudly, "Exactly."

Soften recollects one particular incident. It involves the time he is sent away by his employer the Red Cross because he's wearing trousers. He goes home, puts on a dress and some high heels, and returns. For a week he feels ashamed. Then he decides to have a word with his boss, whom he tells that what he wears has no bearing on the quality of his work. Dresses are for *ladies*, not for lesbian men. The Red Cross is just going to have to get used to it. Not every biological woman is a woman. Full stop.

The football training field is flanked by mountains on one side, and the city's main hospital on the other: a grey, non-descript building of ten floors. One of the players is being treated for a head wound. He'd been defending his lady against a group of youths. The sun is shining; they stop playing, and wet with sweat, they seek shelter under the public grandstand. "You have to show the ladies that they're dealing with a real man," explains the slightly built Brendon. He tells the story of the time that a lesbian woman, one Saturday evening, entered a bar in which one of their own,

Castakes, was the manager. "This woman is wearing a skirt and a little top with thin straps. Her breasts are pushed right up so they're almost bursting out. She then begins to make a pass at one of the girls. In those clothes! That's just not done. You can't wear a skirt and expect to get the girl," Brendon says. His teammates nod in unison. It's true. Just as a woman who is going out with a lesbian man isn't a real lesbian. It doesn't matter what they do in bed. A lady will always be a lady, and ladies are not lesbians. It's a little confusing, as one of us, a visitor from faraway Amsterdam, now qualifies as one. It's a whole new way of looking at things.

The lesbian men of Katutura have been friends for years. When a new lady comes on the scene, they will always ask each other for help and advice. They'll comfort each other if it doesn't work out. Brendon laments the fact that ladies are often so impatient. "You've only just met and all they want to do is pull your clothes off." Take for example his new girlfriend. "I say to her that she needs to take things a little slower. She wants to see me today. Tomorrow she wants me to sleep with her. Saturday and Sunday we're meant to be going to see a film. *Slow down sweetie*, this is all going a bit too fast for my liking. Let's see each other today and then again sometime next week." Now she's mad at him.

It's a different matter in public. In the street, it's his girlfriend who keeps her distance. She's afraid that she'll lose her job if anyone finds out she's having a relationship with Brendon. He can only greet her as though they're just good friends. He finds it tiring.

The lesbian men never tell each other about the ins and outs of their sex lives. That's a private matter. But they do complain about how some ladies want to have sex with a lesbian man just so that they can boast to everyone else about what they've done and what they look like. That's part of the reason they tend to keep their t-shirts on when having sex. They'll make sure the ladies get as much pleasure as possible, but their own pleasure tends to come alone. Because you never know. "There are thousands of others just like us. The problem is that they don't want to be identified. They're only active at night."

*

Day or night, in the dark or out in the open. What has any of it to do with one's sexual preference? "What is not visible is easier to tolerate," argues Farid Esack, the South African theologian, writer and professor of religious studies at the University of Johannesburg. He is a devout Muslim and constantly testing his pupils with his liberal, progressive views. His youth spent in a segregated suburb of Cape Town has been a major influence on his intellectual development. Only coloureds were allowed to live there; those who were the product of forbidden multi-cultural relationships, the descendants of slaves transported to Cape Town, or the original inhabitants of the Cape, the Khoi. He grew up here with his single mother. It was exceedingly poor and smacked of inequality and injustice. His resistance to apartheid lead Esack to be arrested and jailed a number of times. In the 1980s, he emerged as one of the leading figures in the fight for democracy, with the principles of non-racialism an inspiration to many.

This ideology was the cause of fierce debate within the freedom movement in the 1950s. Initially, a large majority, including one Nelson Mandela, took the view that the oppressed should seek revenge for the unjust system they had to endure for so long, and must fight those who profit from it – the whites. Blacks against whites. Others saw the system itself as the target. If apartheid was destroyed, the freedom of whites would also follow, as they would be rid of a superiority enforced by law. In this way blacks could work together with those whites who were seen to uphold the same principles of non-racialism. Mandela was deeply affected in those early years by his experiences with white compatriots who had an equal determination to rid the country of apartheid, and as a consequence became convinced that multiracial cooperation was the way forward. Eventually, thinking in terms of colour alone was dismissed.

It's likely that Esack's constant questioning of the entrenched ideas and prevailing views over identity have evolved as a consequence of his experiences during the anti-apartheid struggle. He refuses to answer questions relating to his own sexual preference, just as archbishop Desmond Tutu, when once asked which race he belongs to, considered it an affront, and answered with "I am South African." Esack's reaction is just as frosty; he asks why would anyone discuss their sexual preference with someone they've only just met. He will come back to this later in our conversation.

What interest is served by revealing such information? There is also a certain strategy behind it. He considers the compulsion to give names to all the different varieties of sexuality as a dilemma for a society in which tradition is held in such high regard. They tend to tolerate what is perceived as abnormal, so long as it is not shoved in their faces and operates under the cover of darkness.

Today's out homosexual is either gay or lesbian, and wants to be identified as such. He or she is no longer content to sit back and allow what is seen as an essential part of their identity being swept under the carpet. People want their sexual preference acknowledged by others. Esack: "They want the rest of society to understand and understand this. They no longer just want a just quick wink and a nudge, but a full acknowledgement over dinner and coffee. Only then will people accept what they are and afford them equal rights." All these determined and overt expressions of sexuality and sexual identity are undermining the unspoken rules that are considered the glue to holding a society together. It's as though LGBT activists have suddenly turned on a light that was turned off long ago by missionaries. In the twilight of the Victorian era, a strict system of standards and values applied, inspired by hundreds of pages of Biblical text relating to good and evil, sin and chastity. It's not clear how widespread homophobia in Africa was before the advent of colonialisation, but what is certain is that the Western occupiers gave it a shot in the arm.

Esack knows from experience that traditional Muslim communities have little tolerance for any light that's shone on the issue of sexuality. As a fifteen-year-old he left South Africa to study in Pakistan and spent nine years studying Islamic law and theology at an institute that would later produce some of the leadership in the Afghan Taliban. One of the rules of the *madrassa*, the religious school, is that the 'beardless boys' are not permitted on the beds of the older students. These and other regulations are set down purely to prevent sex from taking place. "Everyone knows that older men sometimes 'counsel' young boys, but no-one ever says anything." Interestingly, they are not treated with any contempt, and many of these men consider themselves highly traditionalist in their outlook. "I think that traditional societies function when things that may be common can still be regarded in polite discourse as abnormal. Normality becomes normality because the abnormal is not spoken about in the space of the normal," Esack says.

In the Muslim world it's the more enlightened Sufis who ask the thought-provoking questions. "They do their own thing and experience God in music and dance. The power that orthodoxy wields over the lives of ordinary people is threatened by all this. If people start discovering God for themselves, we are out of business, man! Control gives us meaning and to control we must have light; we are afraid of the dark. It really is all about our own power structures." Esack says he is bewildered by the similar inclination the modern gay community has for order. Everyone has a label: gay, lesbian, bisexual, transgender, intersex, queer, tomboy, manwoman, you name it. The lesbian men of Katutura, and their ladies, are an expression of this longing for classification and distinction. It goes hand-in-hand with ghettoisation, *us* against *them*. Esack sees it as an expression of the need for people to belong to something, and to feel safe amongst like minds. But a ghetto tends to endorse a system in which one form takes precedence over another. Ultimately, the ghetto is the safe haven for the underdog. Esack understands the desire for a segregated gay scene. You can be yourself and demonstrate your idiosyncrasy. But this separation keeps the status quo intact. Neighbourhoods where gays, or for example Chinese people, tend to congregate – what is the consequence of this partitioning for society in general? The nurturing of these neighbourhoods allows the majority to feel more comfortable and tolerant of the 'exotic other'. It is this conformity that helps to reinforce the perception of difference.

Esack illustrates the relationship between parochialism and the retention of power with an example from the time the mosque he visited still refused to admit women. "I went to a memorial service. When I walked inside, I came face to face with a woman. She was wearing a t-shirt with a low neckline that clearly showed her breasts. It didn't shock or surprise me. The woman was black and a cleaner. This showed for me the capacity of the mainstream to deal with otherness. Women cannot enter the mosque, cleaners can. It suddenly dawned on me that our community has no difficulty with accepting differences, as long as these 'others' are in a clear position of subordination."

It's this story that sets Esack apart from another leading thinker in the Muslim firmament. Joseph Massad is a professor of modern Arabic politics and intellectual history, and is a self-declared opponent of what he calls *Gay International*, a movement 'dominated by white, Western gay men'. Massad believes that this creates a one-sided, uniform approach to homosexual lifestyles, without room for alternatives. In contrast, the Arab world does not apply a name to homosexuality. But according to Esack, Massad is implying that Muslim communities can deal with homosexuality and have always dealt with it. "But what he doesn't say is: as inferior citizens!" They're tolerated in the same way as the black cleaner in the mosque.

Esack has to laugh at Massad's accusation that Western gays, with their tendency to label themselves as such, disturb the natural harmony that exists in traditional communities. "If this black cleaner starts to organise herself and demands equal rights, does it mean that she's disturbing the harmony between herself and the mosque? Of course she is. The ethical question is: *should* the harmony be disturbed?" Esack cannot answer whether openness about one's sexual preference is the best way to win over a traditional society, but people have "the right to fight for a dignified existence under God's sun". He casts aside the criticism from opponents of equal rights that Western activism is gradually invading the Arab world and other developing countries, and must therefore be immediately suspect. "A lot of bad things have been inflicted on us, as well as a lot of good things. The fight for human rights, against slavery and racism, equality for women – these all have their origin in the West; they're a product of the Enlightenment. All these developments are being embraced by Africa. There is something disingenuous about singling out a particular trend of gay rights or affirming gay identities."

One of the main lines of defence against homophobia is that homosexuality is genetically determined from birth. In other words, there's nothing you can do about it. It's the argument that Archbishop Desmond Tutu always raises when he's trying to convince his religious colleagues that you cannot persecute an individual for something that is given to them by nature. Esack questions this. "They basically argue that this is how God made homosexuals and straights. I don't know. I think that possibly the religious argument can make a case for homosexual versus straight sexuality." But how do you approach a sexuality that can change – a sexuality that leaves you falling for a man at one moment, and then for a woman, and so on? Esack predicts that is likely to be a step too far. "I don't think there's room for the idea that sexuality can be something dynamic, that God is continuously creating and that one of the ways this creation manifests itself is in one's changing sexual orientation." Esack is calling for a serious theological debate. One that challenges preconceived ideas rather than looking for concrete answers. "What does it mean to be an elusive character, one that refuses to fit into any category, in relation to marriage, to the stability of parenthood? That is a much more frightening theological question."

*

The Mozambican writer Mia Couto is also questioning the perceived wisdoms that permeate society. He's known as one of the most original literary voices in the Portuguese language. He finds his expression in magical realism, where reality and fiction are often so intertwined that it's impossible to distinguish one from the other. He likes to view the world with a fresh pair of eyes. Growing up in colonial Mozambique as the son of Portuguese settlers, he saw first-hand how oppression affects people. He broke off his studies in biology to join the freedom movement Frelimo in its fight against the colonial occupier, Portugal. He returned to university after a break of twelve years, and because he was older and white, and therefore somehow the sole possessor of truth and wisdom, he became an oracle in the field of sexuality for his fellow students. "Who should close their eyes during a kiss, the man or the woman?" Couto replies that it doesn't matter, that it's all to do with passion. "Of course, I knew absolutely nothing about it."

Couto goes one step further than Esack and also throws the division between men and women into the melting pot, describing it as not straightforward and no indisputable reality. He considers it a construct, a notion that exists in order to classify our place in the world – something based on centuries of historical and religious preconceptions. A man is on earth to procreate. He has a fixed role in the world, namely to exercise his authority. A woman, in her turn, exists to bear children and to serve. As soon as the sex of the baby has been determined, the role-play begins. And you cannot jump from the ship at will. Whoever questions this division of roles steps over the mark and becomes a threat. Just as Mandela and Esack condemn any rationale based on colour, Couto challenges a strict division of people in men and women. "That is uncomfortable because we are both. That's perhaps why all over the world you have carnival, to create a moment of escape. People can become what they want. The first thing you see happening in countries that are strongly male dominated, is that men disguise and dress themselves as women. It is a real temptation. It looks like a contradiction, strong muscular men who want to act as women. But the reason is this oppressive role we have. For days on end they'll dance in the street and express themselves as a woman. Finally, it's allowed!"

Couto remembers a friend who would always be seen in a dress during the Mozambican carnival. "I made beautiful photos which I showed to him a little while afterwards. He became angry and wanted me to throw them away. He couldn't bear seeing himself as a woman. It seemed really odd because the following year he put on the same clothes again. The law of disorder and chaos can only last for just a few days. Religion, rules of social engagement, traditions - they're all thrown out of the window. I can do what I want and, perhaps, just for a moment *be* who I really am, or who I want to be. There is space, such as there is in dreams, to be free."

Couto compares the strict rules that govern one's behaviour with a theatre – we *play* at being a man and a woman. He thinks it's not an easy role to play. What if we're both, or neither? Couto is not gay himself, but loves the idea of also being a woman. He expresses such feelings in his books. "I'm grateful for literature. It allows me to cross this frontier. When I describe a female persona, I *am* that woman. I have to completely become her in order to tell her story. The journeys of identity, to be black and white, young and old, man or woman, that's what I love. It's my own permanent carnival!"

There are many African LGBT's who are also testing the boundaries of acceptance. They defy prevailing conventions, morality, alleged traditional values, religious convictions and sometimes the very laws of nature. They're not just advocating change, they're an expression of it. They're creating a new set of rules and developing a new morality. It may all seem modern and refreshing, but the rules are just as strictly defined, with a rigidity that bears a striking resemblance to those imposed by their adversaries. The *ladies* and *gents* of Ermelo, a town 250 kilometres east of Johannesburg, apply these rules to the point where fantasy and reality are interchangeable. Fashion plays an important role; a skirt and make-up is *de rigueur* for a real *lady* in 1994, but considered *too much* in 2003.

The South African anthropologist Graeme Reid made frequent visits to Ermelo over a period of two years in an attempt to explain the world of these *gents* and *ladies*. His thesis, 'How to be a real gay?', describes his findings. He observed that femininity and masculinity are magnified as well as subverted. The *gents* in Standerton, Ermelo's township, feel and behave as heterosexual men. The *ladies*, on the other hand, consider themselves homosexual. According to Reid, the difference lies in what you *do*. Cooking, ironing, washing, cleaning, being penetrated – that makes you a *lady*. They do womanly things, both in the house and at work. The *gents* are the *ladies'* boyfriends. They do manly things. They drink, hold their cigarette between their thumb and forefinger, demand that their food is served at the table at the right time, discipline and occasionally beat up their *ladies*. They have multiple sexual partners, *ladies* and women. Everyone has their own role to play and clearly defined daily practices, but it seems to be the *ladies* who have more freedom to blossom and develop.

Reid writes that the sexuality of the *gent* is restricted by a need to conform to the traditional male role, whereas the *ladies* seem to have more scope for modifying and adapting their behaviour in a wider social circle. They're not only economically more successful (with hair salons, for example); some of them, the 'modern, liberated *ladies*', organise workshops on 'how to be a real gay' and talk among themselves about domestic violence, and whether they're really content with sharing their *gents* with heterosexual women. Reid ponders: Is the *lady* no longer a man, or is she one of the ways a man can be?" This philosophical question gets to the very core of his research: is it possible for variations to exist in a man and a woman? The fact that, during his research, a number of *ladies* suddenly transmogrify into *gents*, and one *gent* asks himself whether he might in fact be a *lady*, shows how complicated it is to move effortlessly from one identity to the other and how determinative fixed labels are — for heterosexuals and the LGBT community alike.

The South African photographer and visual artist Zanele Muholi wants people to return to the drawing board and ask themselves: what is gender and what is sexuality? How can it be channelled and who decides it? Muholi is a well-known LGBT activist and has won many prestigious international prizes for her photography. In 2013, she was awarded the Fine Prize for the emerging artist at the Carnegie International, and received the Prince Claus Award in Amsterdam. She has taken thousands of photographs of black lesbians and transgenders in South Africa and elsewhere. Her work demonstrates an anger and abhorrence of the many rapes that take place of lesbian women in her country, juxtaposed with images of self-assured and dignified lesbians and transgender people.

Not everyone is in thrall to her work, such as the previously mentioned politician Lulu Xingwana. In a 2010 exhibition of young black artists in Johannesburg, Xingwana walked out in disgust after having taken a brief look at a photo series from Muholi of naked, lesbian women. "Immoral and against nation building," were her words as she breezed out of the exhibition. Perhaps she had expected to see clothed lesbians. Or quite possibly, no lesbians at all. Muholi is explicit in what she portrays, and provocative. Art should not be easy on the eye, or something to glance at before moving on to the next piece. It has to provoke discussion, ask questions, and evoke a sense of confusion. In 2009, she stands behind a window in

Amsterdam's red light district, wearing just a short beaded skirt. The aim is to deliberately unnerve those walking by. The man *sees* a black prostitute, but Muholi is observing a man who *thinks* he's seeing a prostitute. She's also giving her own community something to think about. A butch lesbian in a skirt? Or standing in a window? "I want people to discuss these issues," she says. "I want them to think more deeply about women and work like prostitution." With this mix of artistry and activism, Muholi is exceeding even her own boundaries. Take the photo series in the red light district. "It's as though I'm someone else. I'm living as another woman, a woman who stands behind a window. I cannot do that in real life, I wouldn't dare be seen in public like that."

Ladies, *gents* and *lesbian men* all make use of traditional gender roles to remodel the unconventional into something ordinary. The Kenyan writer and columnist Binyavanga Wainaina describes it as the creation of a safe zone within a taboo. It's a place where the taboo itself is neither attacked nor criticised, and where one can do as one pleases. A good example is the 'msenge' culture on the coast of Kenya. Msenge is a Swahili word for passive, or an effeminate gay. "Two men who have sex with each other is taboo. But if one of the men is msenge, then it's possible," says Wainaina. Then a man takes his woman home with him. The woman is a man, but you call him her. It's not completely approved of, but there is an acknowledged and defined identity: 'the msenge'. The man who shares his bed with the msenge is not considered homosexual, because the msenge is a woman. The msenge lies, literally and figuratively, under the man. Therefore everything is in order, only a little different. "A lot is possible, as long as one sticks to the unwritten code of secrecy. In cultures like this, vilification and mockery are never far away."

Wainaina wonders what impact Western influenced gay and lesbian movements will have on the msenges. These movements have little time for anything that deviates from the *modus operandi* of identity politics and 'coming out'. Wainaina finds the animosity between these different worlds intriguing. Gay and lesbian movements generally consider the question 'who is the woman and who is the man' an insult. For msenges, it goes to the very core of their existence. However, Wainaina does not believe they should be 'protected' from modern developments. In that way you'd be turning them into an indigenous and fixed group. Perhaps they do want to be different, perhaps they don't. He wants to show it as a manifestation of the gay and lesbian community in all its many colours – first get to know all the different tastes, and then you'll be able to make your choice from what is available. People should be able to make up their own mind whether they want to be called gay and whether they want to come out of the closet. There should be scope to do your own research, weigh up all the options, and then choose. In Nairobi, it's possible to be openly gay in some clubs, hair salons and neighbourhoods, whilst at the same time keeping one's parents completely in the dark. "People live in a sort of bubble," Wainaina says. But it appears that attitudes are shifting slightly. In some of the city's clubs it's seen as a compliment if you're approached by a gay man. It helps to confirm your status as a liberal thinking individual. "I was really surprised when I saw men dancing provocatively with each other. They're trying things out."

Perhaps the biggest legacy of the gay movements in Africa has been, through demanding freedom to be oneself, the opening up of the discussion over distinctions between what is considered normal and abnormal. The feminist movement did the same. "There is nothing much traditional about tradition," says Farid Esack. "It's about trying to legitimate our own control over the lives of other people. It works the same way as with religion." Esack illustrates what he means with a small family anecdote. When his father complains that his daughter-in-law has not made any tea for him, Esack replies by explaining there is nothing in the Koran that offers any guidance in this respect. Nowhere does it state that it is the duty of a partner to provide tea for her husband, let alone for her father-in-law. "If that's the Sharia, the Sharia can go to hell," his father answers – a deeply religious man who prays five times a day.

*

What certainly plays a role in the debate, initiated by the likes of Esack, Couto, Muholi, Reid and Wainaina, are the experiences that have been specific to Africa – especially the fight against colonialism and apartheid. There have been long lasting and very recent histories of divide and rule, ethnic cleansing, social disruption, traumas. It's from these struggles that stories arise of vested interests, recovery, and, sadly, further setbacks. But what does this all mean for the fight being waged by sexual minorities? And what is its impact on the much broader geopolitical stage in Africa? These are the questions with which those in this chapter, and many others, have been occupying themselves. The close interweaving of past and present, the smouldering victimisation, the new dynamism, the injustice that has affected so many on the continent and left so many with scars – irrespective of sexual preference. This all makes Africa *different*.

But it's equally self-evident how the intellectual curiosity of these thinkers shares a common ground with what's happening elsewhere in the world: issues about gender, sexual rights, patriarchal relationships, ghetto formation, identity and so on. Those who make a study of these developments will soon discover certain patterns occurring again and again, regardless of place, country or continent. Sometimes the period in which they happen might be different, and sometimes there are striking parallels. They may be wrapped in different terminology, but whoever takes a moment to delve beneath the veneer of cultural demarcations will recognise the similarities. With this in mind, Africa is *just the same*.

Chapter 5

An obsession extraordinaire

Anglican church leaders in Africa are playing a key role in imposing orthodox teachings on their congregations. The goal: gaining the upper hand over a church dominated by whites. The means: fuelling hatred against homosexuals. South African Archbishop Desmond Tutu thinks his colleagues are spearheading this campaign out of a sense of powerlessness against problems such as poverty, disease and AIDS."We want to feel that we can solve problems. We don't want to look impotent. And so some bishops turn to an issue that looks solvable."

Schism and discord are as old as the church itself. So it comes as little surprise that for the past couple of decades Christian American traditionalists and progressives have been at each other's throats. What *is* new is the way this unseemly struggle within American Protestantism has crossed the Atlantic and penetrated the African continent. There exists within every denomination in the Protestant church a reactionary movement that sets itself against its more mainstream church communities. They're seen as too liberal, too gay friendly, too pro-women – in short, anything that comes too close to the mindset of a secular society. In its place, they're pleading for a more conservative interpretation of the Bible – perhaps even the utopia of a church run state. The conflict has been characterised by the New York Times as "the biggest struggle for the future of American Protestantism since the churches split over the question of slavery during the American civil war".

Whilst it might seem as though the fight for the soul and direction of the church is of overriding concern, it's the more earthly matters of money, power, colour and possessions that are playing just as important a role, albeit behind the scenes. The support base of the Christian right in the US has traditionally come from the southern Baptist regions, but since the end of the 1990s the ranks of those evangelists believing in miracles and exorcism has risen sharply amongst the old school Anglican provinces that predominate in the north. Whole parishes and dioceses are now breaking from the Episcopal Church (the name given to the Anglican church in the US), mainly because of its more progressive attitudes to divisive issues. It blesses same-sex couples and has appointed gay and lesbian bishops, in contravention of the conservative course set down by the Lambeth Conference in 1998. This worldwide 'Anglican parliament' meets every ten years, and its incarnation at the end of the millennium declares, after a passionate debate, that homosexuality is "incompatible with the teachings of the Bible". This declaration is a convincing victory for the orthodox faction within the church, but in a slight nod to the progressives, a decision is taken to create 'listening circles'. In this way, the church can examine the experiences of gays and lesbians. Orthodox leaders interpret this as guiding those lost sheep towards the true path, to make them conscious of their sin, and lead them towards what is normal – heterosexuality. The liberals, on the other hand, see it as a means to continue the debate, and feel a sense of optimism over the call to end the "irrational fear of homosexuality" incorporated into the Conference's final declaration. It's during this debate that many African bishops attending the progressive conference declare themselves fervent opponents of the progressive changes taking root in the US. The American conservative minority has thus assured itself of African support.

The walls of Desmond Tutu's office reception are filled with framed photographs of him rubbing shoulders with world leaders and other famous people. The former Anglican Archbishop of Cape Town, who retired in 1996, is waiting for us at the entrance. His office is light and spacious. Tutu is now in his mid-eighties, but describing him as retired would be a wild inaccuracy. In the intervening twenty years, he has switched regularly between declarations of 'slowing down' and high tempo calls for Israelis to 'free themselves' by allowing the Palestinians their own state, for banks not to invest in companies that threaten the environment, and to anyone who wants to listen – continuing the fight against corruption and abuse of power. Tutu is seen as South Africa's moral conscience. In 2008, he was honoured by the International Gay and Lesbian Human Rights Commission (IGLHRC) for his support for campaigns against discrimination on the grounds of sexual preference.

"It's an extraordinary obsession," is Tutu's reply when asked why the subject of homosexuality is so high on the church's agenda. His condemnation of homophobia is blunt, and he finds the comparison with the politics of apartheid justifiable. "People are being persecuted or discriminated against for something that they can't do anything about: their ethnicity, their skin colour, or their sexual preference." During the apartheid years such public statements about homosexuality were kept in check, with his former bishop convincing him that it was not possible to fight on two separate fronts at the same time. "We were already fighting a major battle within the church itself. When I supported sanctions many white people were very angry with me. And when I became Archbishop of Cape Town in 1986 quite a few left, because *Mister Sanctions*, this awful man who mixes politics with religion, is now our archbishop." But when the battle was finally over and official apartheid was swept aside, Tutu threw his hat into the ring as an outspoken supporter of equal rights for gays and lesbians. In 2008, he pulled no punches, and declared that the struggle could be compared with that against racism. In an interview with *Afrol News,* he argued that a "parent who brings up a child to be a racist damages that child, damages the community in which they live, damages our hopes for a better world. A parent who teaches a child that there is only one sexual orientation and that anything else is evil denies our humanity and their own too. Homophobia is a crime against humanity."

Why does Tutu think that some Anglican church leaders are spearheading the hate campaigns? In his view, it is a feel good exercise. Tutu: "They live in countries that face almost intractable problems, like poverty, corruption, oppression. Often these are not democratic countries. Now all of us want to feel we are making a difference, that we can solve problems. There are so many problems, I am going to look for one that looks solvable, they think. Most of us don't want to seem impotent in the face of these huge problems. And this one seems straight forward, it seems so easy to say: the Bible says homosexuality is wrong. Full stop. But I don't believe that God is so obsessed with the genital activity of men and women. If God is a homophobe, then that is not the God I worship." When asked whether the hate campaigns conducted in the name of the church warrant the establishment of a truth and reconciliation commission, there's a long silence. In the 1990s, Tutu was the chair of such a commission set up to look into the excesses of the apartheid era. He wrestles with the question, weighing up the consequences of what his answer might entail, with newspaper headlines declaring 'Tutu calls for a new truth commission against homophobia in the church'. He cautiously measures his response as follows: "I am sorry that we could be so ostracising, that we could inflict so much anguish and pain and for the rejection that so many of them have experienced."

When South Africa guarantees freedom of sexual preference in its 1996 constitution, the Anglican community is thrust into a dilemma. It must now determine the path it wishes to take. Two years before, Rowan Smith, who was Cape Town's deacon at the time, remembers watching a television debate on the impending constitution with his eight brothers and sisters. When the debate turns to the non-discrimination clause, Smith lets slip: "They're talking about me!" His brothers and sisters are taken aback and ask him what he means. "I just repeated that they weren't talking about someone far away, they were talking about me." A week later he lets Archbishop Desmond Tutu into his confidence. "He'd already suspected something," Smith says, "Probably because of my enthusiasm during discussions about rights for gays and lesbians."

Tutu remembers the conversation. "Yes, I was aware of it. Two of my chaplains were gay. One of them was the dean and he came out, and the other one has become a bishop. It was known in the church and when he was elected, at one point somebody raised the issue of his sexuality. It was incredible. An older white priest said: 'We don't care about his sexuality, we just want to know if he will take good care of us.' It was one of the most wonderful times, when I presided over the National Assembly where he won and got elected."

After Smith's 'coming out', he's invited to give a sermon in Cape Town's cathedral on marriage and the recognition of marriage for homosexuals. "I talked about the recognition of 'our' relationships. The following day the editor of the local newspaper asked: 'Did the deacon say *we*?' It was then that I gave an interview and came completely out of the closet."

Smith was full of praise for the way *his* bishop spoke about equal rights. "Tutu was becoming increasingly outspoken," he remembers. "One particular moment he said: 'To accept gay people but not their relationships, is like saying it's okay to be a bird, but you mustn't fly.' Goodness gracious, something happened!" He thinks it's a pity that Tutu stepped down as archbishop before the 1998 Lambeth conference, believing that his presence there would have greatly improved the chances of a more favourable outcome. Smith is witness to how differently the declaration taken at Lambeth has been interpreted within the Anglican community.

In Uganda, for example, church leaders may wish to offer their blessings to homosexual believers, but if a miraculous cure fails to materialise, and certainly if there's no wish for any healing, then connections are immediately curtailed. The Anglican church in Uganda is playing an active role in the campaign for a sharpening of the anti-gay laws. It's different in the US where a majority of Anglicans view homosexuality, as well as the maintaining of a homosexual relationship, as no obstacle to a career within the church. It's a tough task for the global leadership of the church, by tradition centred in Canterbury in England, to hold both sides together. The current Archbishop of Canterbury Justin Welby, as his predecessor Rowan Williams, has been openly admonished by a defiant conservative faction for seemingly tolerating the homosexual consecrations taking place in Canada and the US. The Anglican community has always been a faith for those who wish to incorporate both Protestant *and* Catholic philosophies. It therefore allows for a mixed bag of different, sometimes contradictory, directions and opinions. The conservative minority wants to alter this fundamental premise and bring the whole issue to a head by speeding towards a collision course with every form of pluralism. They view a strict interpretation of the Bible as the only truth, and demand sanctions on those dioceses that are exploring the boundaries of their autonomy. So they're insisting on the right to kick out quirky, progressive minded church communities from the global Anglican fraternity. This can't be done with the backing of Britain or the United States, so they're looking for support elsewhere, mainly in the southern hemisphere.

In 2003 there is a new set back for the conservative faction when the diocese of New Hampshire elects Robinson as its new bishop coadjutor, making him the first openly gay bishop in the Episcopal Church. It has taken many years but finally, a US diocese is willing to nail its colours to the church spire. Liberals celebrate a famous victory and Robinson travels around the world giving talks to packed houses. Not surprisingly, the announcement is met with incredulity and anger by conservatives, and it's the catalyst for new ruptures and developments. The row leads to several major shifts. The phenomenon of the 'offshore bishop' makes its entrance. American parishes with a conservative majority are removed from the supervision of the Episcopal Church and placed under the authority of an overseas bishop. This bishop then delegates his authority back to conservative Anglican networks in the US, such as the American Council. It's initially seen as a temporary measure, to remain in place until the orthodox philosophy becomes, once more, the dominant force in the US. It's an ingenious move. Suddenly, a minority conservative movement in the US is overseeing millions of the African faithful. The American conservatives have thus increased their influence exponentially. And there's a belief that they can use this sudden 'multiplication' of their flock to prevent any further liberal developments within the church. The second development is the establishment in 2008 of an organisation that's seen as a direct challenge to the Lambeth Conference. It's called the Global Anglican Future Conference (GAFCON) - a few hundred conservative bishops meet in Jerusalem and set up this new worldwide network, with its own headquarters from where interdenominational obstruction can be coordinated and acted upon.

Deacon Rowan Smith is conscious of a growing alliance between US conservatives and like-minds in Africa even before the 1998 Lambeth Conference. One of the first instances of this growing realisation is a meeting in the Africana Hotel in Kampala between Ugandan church leaders and representatives from the American neo-conservative think-tank, the Institute on Religion and Democracy (IRD). "It was here that they chose to go down the route of being more judgemental, in contrast to the many preceding years in which understanding and compassion had taken precedence," Smith says. The acceptance of homosexuality was quickly deemed the most suitable issue on which to confront the liberals head-on. However, the roots of this resistance have their origin in the 1970s, when the first calls come to appoint women into the service of the church. "But in that time there was an understanding that one could agree to differ," Smith notes. "Today it seems that when it comes to homosexuality, there's only one interpretation."

What at first glance seems like a struggle for the 'true path' is in reality a power struggle. American money and the sheer numbers of African believers have become seamlessly melded. Smith: "The conservatives claim the Anglican church in Nigeria has seventeen million followers and if so, then it's more than all the Anglicans put together in the northern hemisphere." It's the reason many believe the focus of power should shift towards the south, and why conservative dissidents describe it as the 'global south'. After decades of navigating between the margins of society, American Christian fundamentalists are enjoying a new lease of life, with the help of their conservative African allies.

Trevor Mwamba, who was the bishop of Botswana until 2013, thinks the vast majority of Africans have more important things to do than to care too much about homosexuality and whether it's acceptable or not. In his mini-office next to the Anglican church in the centre of Gaborone, he tells us about the social and economic problems that many Africans are dealing with. "These are the issues that we find important and which determine our priorities." And the appointment of Gene Robinson? Mwamba answers by saying that people aren't looking at his sexual preference, but at his qualities as a bishop. He also understands why American conservatives now have their sights set on Africa. "They view Robinson's appointment as a big defeat. So the power struggle continues. As soon as the conservatives in the US realise that they have lost the battle, they start an international war with a further jump across the border into Africa." Mwamba also accuses the conservatives of hijacking the debate over homosexuality that's taking place in the media. "You need a good enough topic to define the positions within the church. And this has become an ideal tool." The highly vocal Anglican bishops of Nigeria, Uganda, Rwanda and Kenya are all, according to Mwamba, conscripts in an American mercenary war. "Nigeria is just *one* church province, but it has a really strong militant approach. The church provinces further south in Africa are much more numerous, and take a more liberal position. The main reference points here are that we are all God's children and there's a lot that still has to be discussed and investigated." Mwamba's own church province, Central Africa, falls between the two. "People think primarily that homosexuality is incompatible with the teachings of the Bible, and wrestle with the fact that any answer will not be easily forthcoming. We believe in a fellowship that allows for extremes, and don't want to force anyone into a straightjacket." Mwamba believes this is the compassion that reflects the original philosophy of the Anglican church. He laments its fragmentation and the emergence of a vociferous group of 'extremists', and asks: "Debates about homosexuality and who we can go to bed with? Was Jesus at all engaged with this issue? We're completely losing sight of what the church is all about. The history of Africa is repeating itself. Once again it's become the battleground for other people's war," he says – a pointed reference to the Cold War that cost Africa so dear.

In 2008, Mwamba comes into conflict with the Zimbabwean bishop Nolbert Kunonga. This chum of president Mugabe is one of the beneficiaries of the government's policy of confiscating land owned by white farmers, and dishing it out to its allies. Kunonga's rewards are considerable, and he subsequently uses any means possible to resist all attempts by the former owners to retrieve their property. Kunonga also attempts to remove his Harare diocese from the control of the Central Africa church province, saying that, under Mwamba's leadership, it has "become homosexual". As a consequence he would be able to appropriate church property and strengthen his own position, but he overestimates his powers. The church rejects these concerns and forces him to resign. It doesn't help his cause when, prior to any decision, he barricades himself inside the capital's cathedral with 40 members of Mugabe's youth militia.

Conservative Anglicans, together with Methodists, Baptists, Presbyterians and Evangelicals, make up a broad alliance of rebels within the Protestant movement.

According to the Zambian researcher, columnist and priest Kapya Kaoma, it's the Institute on Religion and Democracy (IRD) that coordinates the work of the conservatives within the Protestant movement. The IRD was established in 1981 as an alternative to the liberal National Council of Churches, and skilfully weaves together the combined forces of money, people and continents. Every new division occurring within the compass of the Protestant movement seems to have two constants: homosexuality as the catalyst for the protests, and the IRD. According to Kaoma, in order to share resources and strategies, the IRD has managed to bring together conservative groups from each denomination that weren't previously connected. In an IRD report dated from 2004, one can read how three action groups are set up relating to three of the denominations: the Methodists, the Anglicans, and the Presbyterians. Their aim is to ensure that "the conservative lobby gains momentum at all future Conferences". The action group Episcopal Action is requested to work harder on helping change the course of its own church, seen by the IRD as the most liberal of the denominations. The organisation also has high hopes for the increasing number of contacts it's making with orthodox Anglican churches in both Africa and Asia. These are contacts made via their local parishes and mission groups. The leaders of the conservative movements within the Protestant church have, in the meantime, united to form the Association for Church Renewal. The IRD is responsible for PR and for carrying out its agenda.

Kaoma describes how the Evangelicals are skilfully playing on Africa's sensitivity for anything that smacks of a 'neo-colonial agenda'. They've been successful in framing the call for equal rights for homosexuals as part of an attempt to "undermine African values" and as "an expression of arrogance and Western imperialism" – phrases taken directly from the documents of the conservative lobby groups. It's a tactic almost identical to that deployed by conservative African church leaders, and, according to Kaoma, the American fundamentalists have gained a much stronger foothold, with quicker results, in more authoritarian countries such as Uganda, than in those with a stronger mainstream civil society, such as in Kenya.

But many African bishops need little support or encouragement from conservative circles in America to speak out against 'Western domination' in their church. After all, the Anglican church arrived in Africa in the wake of British colonial control. Archbishop Desmond Tutu sums it all up in one, quoting an unknown source: "When the missionaries came to Africa, they had the Bible and we had the land. They said: 'Let us pray.' We closed our eyes. When we opened them, we had the Bible, and they had the land!"

"Why should an Englishman be the boss of our church?" It's this rhetorical question the Ugandan bishop David Zac Niringiye asks when calling for an open discussion over the British leadership of his church. His colleague, the former Archbishop of Kampala Henry Luke Orombi, had already previously announced the "end of the long night of British hegemony". Uganda, after Nigeria, is the biggest Anglican province in the world. "It's clear that the younger churches will shape the Anglican identity," Orombi says. The agendas of the Christian right in the US and conservative church leaders in Africa show clear similarities. But despite being obvious bedfellows, the Africans have their own clearly defined motives for speaking out against Western dominance. Participating in the anti-gay lobby serves their own hunger for power politics, and compensates for a feeling of being humiliated in a white controlled church. It also diverts attention from its own failings and issues of corruption, as well as creating the impression that, with its witch-hunt against homosexuals, it at least has power over something. With Tutu in mind, one could say that the fight against gays is the 'Viagra' African church leaders swallow in order to get themselves worked up about something. On top of that, an attractive supplement to the basic salary of African vicars might be offered, via the collecting tin of their American churchgoers.

Alison Barfoot works at the office of the archbishop in Kampala. This smiley American is an employee of the Ugandan church. She's not in the slightest inconvenienced by the unannounced guests, and agrees without hesitation to a chat with us. She talks freely, but is careful not to give much away. Why has she landed up in Africa? Ah, that's not really a question but, no misunderstandings, it's wonderful here. She finds her work very rewarding. The conclusions of the Zambian researcher Kapya Kaoma, however, show that she's actually controlling the purse strings of the foreign donations of the Christian right, money that is completely hidden from any outside scrutiny by accountants. And the message that she's busy spreading, with a little help from the money that she directs, can be seen in a strategy paper she co-authored in March 2004. It reads that there is a "growing necessity" among American Anglicans to adopt alternative congregations in Africa. The paper calls for the establishment of an overseas AEO (Alternative Episcopal Oversight) that joins forces with North American churches and dioceses, until the control of the church is recaptured and an orthodox reading of the Bible is once again elevated to its rightful position. In this way, these churches will fall under the jurisdiction of the African Anglican church – a church that will have control over all appointments. The consequence, the paper states, will be the gradual transfer of power away from the hands of the liberal dominated church community.

Will she eventually succeed? God only knows.

Chapter 6

All welcome: porn in the church!

At the end of 2013, the Ugandan parliament voted in favour of sharpening the country's anti-gay laws, a decision overturned six months later in the Constitutional Court. The American Christian right is heavily involved in the promotion of homophobia in Africa. This new missionary zeal has other purposes too, such as the hunt for the warlord Joseph Kony, the fight for natural resources, and the 'war on terror'. Ugandan campaigners are reluctant to be seen as mere puppets of a foreign agenda; their own interests are paramount. But does this warrant the screening of gay porn in the church?

There's cheering and chanting as Rebecca Kadaga arrives at Entebbe's airport. The speaker of Uganda's parliament has just returned from a trip to Canada and is being welcomed home as a hero by her supporters. Standing centre stage are the pastor Martin

Ssempa and the former minister for Ethics and Integrity, James Nsaba Buturo, the organisers of this jubilant reception. It is Monday 29 October 2012, and tourists arriving at the airport gaze in amazement at placards declaring: "Uganda sovereign country" and "You are our saviour, we want the bill now!" Who is it that is threatening Uganda's independence? And what law are they referring to?

The backdrop to this rousing welcome is an official visit Kadaga has just made to Canada. Whilst there, she is lectured on the importance of human rights by Canada's minister of foreign affairs, John Baird, and how it also applies unconditionally to homosexuals. It's the umpteenth time a Western country has wagged a finger at Uganda's wayward homophobic policies, which reaches a climax with the Anti-Homosexuality Bill (AHB), originally introduced as a private member's bill by the firebrand politician David Bahati in 2009. Bahati is also at the airport waiting to greet his colleague.

Same sex sexuality is already a punishable offence in Uganda; no new law is required for that. But the new bill will ratchet up the oppression considerably. Every contact "with the intention of performing a homosexual act" will be punishable. The 'victims' of homosexuals are promised anonymity and protection if they report it. It's carte blanche for arbitrary accusations and the settling of old scores. The "promotion of homosexuality" is also prohibited. This goes to the very heart of the proposed new law. Furthermore it becomes an offence to knowingly withhold relevant information from the authorities. Family members or friends who are aware of someone's homosexuality are legally obliged to come forward. The landlord of a LGBT who is renting a property also runs the risk of prosecution. All these crimes are punishable with long jail sentences, and the crowd at the airport fully endorses them.

Kadaga acknowledges her supporters, revelling in the media attention her visit to Canada has brought and the way she has handled the Canadian minister's preaching. She describes Baird's speech as an assault on her country's sovereignty. The colonial era is now over, she says, and no one is in a position to explain to her anything about human rights. The result is a hero's welcome.

Emboldened by all the attention, Kadaga lays down the gauntlet. She swears to do everything in her power to make sure the bill makes a speedy and successful trajectory through the Ugandan parliament. She will teach her foreign critics a lesson and win around heavyweight home-grown opponents of the new law, such as Prime Minister Amama Mbabazi and President Yoweri Museveni. "Here is a woman with a mission, our very own Joan of Arc," one local journalist writes, caught up in the drama and enthusiasm of Kadaga's arrival back home.

Kadaga's stirring words are not just a knee-jerk response to what she considers an affront to her dignity in far-off Canada. This is an ambitious politician with one eye on the future presidency. A 2012 poll suggests that many Ugandans view her as a potential successor to Museveni. The former Anglican Archbishop Henri Luke Orombi, a fervent supporter of the anti-gay law, has already made it clear that the next leader of the country must be a woman. Who else but Kadaga can he be referring to? Nevertheless, it's a breathtakingly hypocritical preference, as the Anglican Church has threatened to implode in the previous decades as a result of two highly contentious issues: permitting women to become bishops and the attitude towards homosexuality. Orombi is firmly in the so-called 'Global South' camp, resistant to all progressive developments and constantly on the lookout for support from members of the ruling elite who could strengthen its position.

Kadaga belongs to this elite. She's not only the speaker of the Ugandan parliament, a position she has held since 2011. She is also, since September 2013, the chair of the Commonwealth Women Parliamentarians, a post she procured in the wake of a recommendation from South Africa. It increases her influence far beyond the borders of her own country. This dual role, some commentators suggest, will force her to dampen any enthusiasm for the new anti-gay law despite her acknowledged sympathies for it. After all, anyone holding these two high profile posts simultaneously should be seen to uphold a semblance of impartiality, and not abiding by this unwritten code of conduct runs the risk of undermining their own position. But Kadaga has other ideas. Driven by the desire for even greater things, she takes another tack. She sees the anti-gay campaign as a vote winner.

One year later. On the afternoon of 18 December 2013, the telephone rings in Martin Ssempa's home.

It is David Bahati from Parliament. "We are going ahead, in two days," he tells the pastor in the strictest of confidence. "The president doesn't know. We're just calling a few people. Don't tell anyone otherwise the whole plan might misfire." Bahati intends to introduce the vote on his anti-gay bill just before the Christmas recess. Ssemba is excited. Finally, it's going to happen. The last few years flash before him – the demonstrations, the church services, the press conferences, his sustained warning of the "collapse of fundamental morals and cultural values". He has pulled everything out of his own closet to make sure that homosexuals remain firmly locked in their own. Now the day of reckoning had arrived and God's work will be rewarded. "Fantastic," is Ssempa's reply. "I'll not say a word."

Forty-eight hours later, a comfortable majority of the parliamentarians present in the house vote in favour of the AHB. Kadaga has fulfilled her promise. As speaker of the house, it's her responsibility to bring a parliamentary motion to a vote, and like a magician pulling a rabbit out of a hat, she announces the vote will take place even though it's not on the day's formal agenda. Prime Minister Mbabazi has just left the debating chamber and is unsuspectingly walking through the building's walkways when he hears over the loudspeakers that Kadaga has called for a vote on the AHB. He angrily storms back into the chamber and demands the proceedings be brought to a halt. "I knew nothing of this ... there are still many questions to be considered ... there is no quorum," he cries. His words are shouted down. Some of his own ministers join in. The proponents of the law, and that includes members of the ruling party, as well as many from the opposition, are no longer willing to see the decision further impeded, quorum or not. Mbabazi tries in vain to invoke the Rules of Procedure, but Kadaga will not be bullied. She says the government has had more than enough time for consultation. Numerous parliamentarians roar in approval, scenting victory. There's clapping and chanting. The two authors of the bill, Bahati and Benson Obua-Ogwal, seem to be glowing with delight. The Prime Minister leaves the chamber with his tail between his legs. This is a man who also carries the unspoken ambition of becoming the president's successor. Today, he's seen himself indubitably trumped by Kadaga.

Asked for his reaction to the outcome by a local journalist, Bahati declares: "This is the perfect Christmas gift we could give Ugandans. I want to thank the speaker for her courage that led to the passing of the bill." He confirms that the vote did not spring out of nowhere, but had been planned in the deepest secrecy. Pastor Ssempa explains it further. "If we had let it out, we couldn't have handled the resistance of gay activists. By this time, this place would be flooded by whites resisting the law." That had indeed been the case over the previous four years, with immediate protests from black gay groups in Uganda and the international community whenever an announcement was made of a forthcoming vote on the issue.

An equally fierce battle was also raging behind the scenes between the pros and antis within Uganda's ruling elite. But the issue of human rights was seldom heard. Those against the bill were playing a more tactical game, with the president declaring "this bill is keeping me from my work."

If it wasn't Hillary Clinton on the phone, it was David Cameron, and once again the issue was shoved back on to the agenda. Documents published by WikiLeaks in September 2011 show President Museveni and his wife Janet totally at odds with each other. Official notes taken from a private meeting between the President's senior advisor John Nagenda and the US ambassador to Uganda, Jerry Lanier, quote the latter as saying that, while the President held a negative image of homosexuality, it is the First Lady, whom he describes as "a very extreme woman", who is ultimately behind the bill. Further leaked diplomatic communiqués show that President Museveni assured American diplomats he would not allow the bill to be passed: "There is someone in Uganda who is handling the matter." That someone is himself. He warns against too much outside interference, saying it will create a new upwelling of public outrage. "Don't push it, I'll handle it," he states. In another leaked document the minister of foreign affairs is quoted as saying, as early as January 2010, that the AHB will eventually die a slow death.

It's a miscalculation and a gross underestimate of the determination of the bill's supporters. But there are important issues on President Museveni's mind other than the threat coming from Western countries to stop foreign aid if he goes ahead and puts his signature on the new law. There is a presidential election to think about in 2016. The president has to weave a delicate course between the two camps, offering hope to both sides in equal measure. At first, he offends the supporters of the law during a parliamentary debate. He asks the rhetorical question whether anybody who deviates from the norm should be locked up. For some Ugandans, Kadaga might fall into this category. She is 58 years old, has never married, and has no children. A little while later, he declares his intention to back the law, but he would set up a ministerial committee containing many scientists that must first determine whether homosexuality is innate or learned. If it's innate, the President says, it would be unjust to make it punishable. Museveni seems to be responding to a petition published by a hundred scientists from around the world concluding there is little doubt within scientific circles that homosexuality has a genetic origin. The former Archbishop of Cape Town, Desmond Tutu, also throws his hat into the ring. In a telephone conversation with Museveni, he makes clear his view that homosexuality is innate and that you can't prosecute people for something they can do nothing about. Tutu also tells the President that homophobia is tantamount to Apartheid and even Nazism, as though it's not enough to just make the comparison with a system of legal discrimination with which South Africa had struggled for so long. He asks Museveni not to sign.

The committee of inquiry concludes its work within a week. It *seems* to state that homosexuality is not innate but a learned condition. It's music to the ears of those wanting more stringent anti-gay laws. Museveni declares he is now ready to sign but, anticipating

Western sanctions, leaves a window slightly ajar. In a press release that is clearly aimed at President Obama, he asks himself whether, now that it's been established that it's not one gene responsible for homosexuality, it might be a combination of genes. If that's the case, "then we can review legislation". Or it might be that Museveni is covering himself against possible repercussions following revelations from the South African *Mail & Guardian* newspaper that appear just two days before he's due to sign. "Uganda MPs falsified gay report," the newspaper reports. It claims that some of the information in the original report written by the scientists had been twisted. The scientists had written "homosexuality has no clear-cut cause and is not a disease or an abnormality", and that there are various factors and these differ per individual. Museveni claims, however, that a different conclusion has been presented to him: "Homosexuality is not a disease but merely an abnormal behaviour which may be learned through experiences in life." The scientists in the commission claim they have been exploited, but all to little effect. A few days later, on Monday morning 24 February 2014, he passes the AHB into law. "Today, I am officially illegal," tweets Kasha Nabagesera, a well-known lesbian activist in Kampala.

Earlier in the month, on 8 February, and two years before the next presidential election was due to take place, a section of Museveni's National Resistance Movement (NRM) proposes, out of the blue, that he should be its sole presidential candidate. It's the perfect tactic to test the loyalty of his parliamentary colleagues and root out his opponents. A vote would mean they would have to remain seated whilst supporters rose from their chairs. It's too much of a political gamble to be seen to be openly rebellious and so, as the vote takes place, Museveni looks on approvingly as, one by one, all his colleagues rise to show their allegiance. Party unity has been restored, potential successors have been chased back into their pens, and his candidacy becomes fact. However, for the first time in his 28 years as president, there is competition for the top post within the party. Prime Minister Mbabazi is also the Secretary-General of the party, and many of its members hold positions thanks to his patronage. There's also whispering behind the scenes that the correct procedures weren't followed during the vote, putting its validity into question. In order to press home who is boss, Museveni sacks his Prime Minister later that year, and the infighting becomes an open struggle when Mbabazi announces his own candidature for the 2016 election, saying he wants to bring "new life into our system of government." But Mbabazi doesn't succeed. With the official results strongly contested by opposition candidates and international observers, Museveni wins the elections in February 2016.

On 24 February 2014, television cameras record the moment a resolute leader puts his name to a law declaring the abhorrence of homosexuality. It's a law Museveni sees little use for, but it satisfies his opponents within the party. When a storm of international protest is unleashed, and Uganda's main gay movement and its allies take their concerns to the Constitutional Court, Museveni's trusted aids, in talks with representatives from Western governments, tell them there's nothing to get too worked up about. The law may well have been passed, but it would not be used in practice; a policy of turning a blind eye would be implemented. In July 2014, the Constitutional Court declares the new law invalid on procedural grounds. A few days later President Museveni is in Washington taking part in a meeting of African leaders, and when back in his own country he declares he doesn't want to antagonise his 'international friends', and he tells parliament any new bill must not be rushed through. The next draft has to be watered down: "At the end of the day, what we really want is just that the 'promotion' of homosexuality is banned," he says. "What people do at home is their own business." And so the President's topsy-turvy approach continues. Meanwhile, gay activists celebrate the Constitutional Court's decision as a victory, even though it's only made on procedural grounds. The outcome, of what has taken on the character of a war of attrition, is still far from assured.

*

"Hello, my name is Scott Lively. I have a brother and sister that went into homosexuality. I have one other sister that wasn't able to enter into marriage until she was in her forties, because of the pain of the family life we had. I know of these things personally. I know more about this than almost anyone in the world." It is Saturday 7 March 2009 and the third day of the conference 'Exposing the Truth behind Homosexuality and the Homosexual Agenda'. Location: the four-star Triangle Hotel in the heart of Kampala. Among those taking part are ministers, civil servants, religious leaders, self-styled messengers from God, and civilians scared of the 'homosexual invasion' their leaders are so often speaking about. The Zambian researcher Kapya Kaoma is also there. He makes secret recordings of everything that's being discussed. Later in the year he publishes his findings in a much-discussed report entitled *Globalizing the Culture Wars: US Conservatives, African Churches and Homophobia*, and places the responsibility for the surge in homophobia in Uganda on the American Christian right.

Sitting on the rostrum at the conference, Scott Lively wears a light yellow shirt with short sleeves. He's a radical preacher from Massachusetts, one of the most liberal states in the US where, since 2004, and thanks to the intervention of the High Court, marriage for homosexuals is permitted. He continues his story to a captive audience: "The fact of the matter is: every single person is heterosexual. That is the design of the human body. A homosexual is a heterosexual person who, when he receives the impulse to have sex, instead of turning to the person he is designed to mate with, he turns to the opposite direction, to the person he is not supposed to mate with." He then goes on to describe how that works in practise so the audience can understand exactly what he means. He turns, so that one side is facing the audience – *that* is the correct design. He waits a while and demonstratively turns 180 degrees. Exactly – *that* is the wrong design. He also knows why people are homosexuals. There are three very clear causes: as a consequence of sexual abuse, from a desire to rebel against authority (often seen in dysfunctional families), and a confusion over gender. According to Lively, the latter happens in early childhood: "These are the people, when they say 'I was born that way', they usually believe that." Lively continues explaining that "after approximately 18 months, a person becomes aware that there are two kinds of people: a mummy and a daddy. Then you decide which one you are. And if the daddy is a distant figure, an alcoholic, the little boy thinks: 'Oh no, I can't be like him, I must be like mummy.' And in this way one becomes homosexual."

The core of his argument is that what you've learnt, can be unlearnt. For example, one can receive therapy such as that offered by another American participant at the conference, Don Schmierer. He's a board member of Exodus International, an organisation that attributes homosexuality mainly to abuse during the early development of the child. Caleb Lee Brundidge is the third speaker from the US to take part. He's an 'ex-gay' who tells those present that a cure is within reach if you want it enough.

Scott Lively escaped the family nest as a damaged individual. One can read on his website how his father was admitted into a psychiatric clinic, and how he himself became addicted to alcohol and drugs at the age of twelve, wandered aimlessly through forty-eight states, slept under bridges, and at the age of sixteen found God in a rehabilitation centre. Lively coined the term "the global gay agenda" and is the co-author of *Pink Swastika*, a book in which he claims the leaders of the Nazi movement were homosexual and that violent fascism is the "natural consequence of the homosexual agenda". Homosexuals are not only the cause of the Holocaust, but also gave a helping hand to Rwanda's genocide, he claims. Lively warns that the US and Europe are both staring destruction in the face. The causes: pornography, abortion, and divorce. Homosexuals are a constant menace, always there behind the scenes, stoking the fire with their immoral behaviour. Lively's fantasy knows no bounds. He can identify twenty-six sexual orientations, with preferences as diverse as children, animals, and shoes. This is a man who sees his mission as preventing the world's lawmakers from falling into the abyss of decriminalising homosexuality. Otherwise, the portals of hell will open, paedophiles will be released into the world, and all animals will be on the run. Type Scott Lively into Google and thousands of documents will take you into a world full of conspiracy theories and associated perversities. It's a veritable handbook of hate. But why does anyone take him seriously?

Lively has a good nose for finding the right places to spout forth his ideas. These are generally dictatorial or lawless states where dislocation, powerlessness and corruption form a breeding ground for people with an inclination towards deceit. That he's taken seriously may be due to the publicity his campaigns receive. His 'Abiding Truth Ministries' always comes near the top of the 'Hate List' of extreme groups compiled annually by the Southern Poverty Law Centre in the US. Lively's approach is simple: gays prey on children, they make victims in every school ground, and must be stopped. It's exactly the line the Ugandan tabloid *Red Pepper* takes in the months following the conference in Kampala. Day after day the newspaper obsessively campaigns against 'this evil among us'. It publishes the names of, at first, fifty gays, lesbians and transgenders, and then two hundred. Included with each name is a photo and address, the name of their partner, the type of car they drive, and their place of work. One of those who appears on the front page is the well-known activist David Kato. In January 2011, he is murdered in his own home by a man who smashes his head with a hammer.

The conference is the culmination of the co-operation between fundamentalist Christians in both Uganda and the US. The American keynote speakers are invited by Stephen Langa, who together with the pastor Martin Ssempa and the self-proclaimed apostle Julius Peter Oyet, form a vociferous trio operating outside the confines of the Ugandan parliament. Who are these three men and how are they connected?

Stephen Langa is the director of the 'Family Life Network' and a board member and elder of the Pentacostal Watoto Church in Kampala headed by pastor Gary Skinner, a man described in numerous publications as one of the most homophobic people in the world. Since the 1990s, Langa has also been associated with the American organisation Disciple Nations Alliance (DNA) in Phoenix. In 2000, it organised its first so-called 'Vision Conference' in Uganda, with the aim of "replacing the African world view with a Bible world view". The Watoto church's aim is to set in motion a 'transformation process' and establish so-called 'cells'. DNA is full of praise for Langa's work. Its website states that his religious influence is widely felt inside Uganda – in government, the family, and the police force. His Watoto is viewed as "truly a model church".

Before there's even time to assess the success of the first conference, Langa announces another meeting hot on its heels, and reads out some malign extracts from Lively's *Pink Swastika*. At a press conference afterwards, he introduces an 'ex-homo' who, it's later revealed, has been well paid for his contribution. He also takes the opportunity to reveal the identities of a number of high-ranking Ugandans whom he accuses of being members of a secret international homosexual conspiracy with – guess what? – a predilection for Ugandan school children.

Langa is on a roll. New accusations follow, together with a call for a mass arrest of homosexuals. Radio FM, a popular station in the country, gives him as much airtime as he wants. Lively keeps everyone informed via his blog. He's delighted with the "clear improvement of the moral climate" in Uganda, and proudly describes the results of his missionary work as "a nuclear bomb on the gay agenda". What's happening in Uganda does not go unnoticed in the US and questions start to be asked in the media that force the Disciple National Alliance to respond to the criticism. At a press conference, Langa is described as a "highly valued colleague" who is expressing his own opinions which don't necessarily reflect those of the DNA. The organisation says "it is no supporter of the criminalisation of homosexuality", but emphasises its continued resistance to the normalisation of homosexuality in schoolbooks.

The DNA is not alone in its attempts to transform a 'derailed and immoral society'. It has been joined by a whole series of like-minded and interlinked organisations. Amongst them we find the International Transformation Network (ITN). Uganda's First Lady Janet Museveni is one of its prominent members. Homosexuals are described as 'possessed by the devil'. There's a strong conviction that praying can help against AIDS.

Julius Peter Oyet can be considered one of the most influential evangelical leaders in Uganda. He makes no secret of being a member of the committee that prepared the anti-gay law, and can hardly conceal his pride during a television interview in 2010 when he proclaims: "I am part of the brains behind it." Oyet is one of the leaders of the New Apostolic Reformation (NAR), a worldwide network founded in 2001 by the American Peter Wagner. At its helm are a number of self-proclaimed apostles and prophets who advocate the 7 Mountains Mandate. The aim is to gain control of seven main areas of society: business, government, religion, family, media, education, and entertainment. Where better than Uganda to realise these goals? Kampala is built on seven hills and its president goes by the nickname of M7 (M-seven-i). Uganda has a destiny to fulfil. Christians must have dominion over every aspect of life, with the ultimate goal of the creation of a theocratic state.

The influence of fundamentalist groups such as the NAR tends to escape close scrutiny due to the loose, seemingly informal, cluster of thousands of churches and related apostle movements. The exponential growth of evangelical mega-churches in Africa, such as the five million strong congregation of the Redeemed Christian Church of God in Nigeria (a country that has also seen a strengthening of anti-gay laws), can be partly attributed to the NAR. The 7 Mountains theology, also known as Kingdom Now, has also taken root within the Republican populist right-wing Tea Party movement in the US.

Oyet maintains warm relations with the American Lou Engle of 'The Call' who organises huge public prayers in the US and calls for a spiritual war against anti-Christian laws such as the legalisation of same-sex marriage. In 2010, Engle takes part in a mass prayer service on the sports fields of Makerere University in Kampala. It's here that Oyet warns parliament not to "debate heaven". Engle follows by declaring he's "no supporter of violence against homosexuals" but sees it as inevitable that the people of Uganda are beginning to turn their backs on "a foreign agenda". Why? Because homosexuality damages society.

Once back in the US, Engle re-emphasises that he does not support the proposed legal changes in Uganda. Oyet responds with a shrug of his shoulders: "He can say whatever he wants to the media but when he was here he said – Uganda, you are key, you are standing now as a leader, for righteousness." That can only be interpreted as support, Oyet concludes.

Oyet is also a key leader of the Born Again Federation, an umbrella movement of the estimated ten thousand evangelical churches in Uganda, the heads of which are dominated by apostles of the NAR. It's due to this position that Oyet is asked to become part of the National Task Force on the Homosexuality Bill, with the task of mobilising the support of religious leaders and raising funds for a national campaign against homosexuality. The agenda of a few zealots must have the appearance of a spontaneous grass roots initiative. It works. In April 2011, Oyet and Ssempa, the two chairs of the Task Force, hand in a petition supporting the proposed law to the speaker of the house, Rebecca Kadaga. At least two million Ugandans have signed it.

Oyet's long list of accomplishments includes his leadership of the 'Lifeline Ministries'. Christine Ondoa, who in May 2011 becomes the country's health minister, is one of its affiliated pastors. Oyet has long suspected that God has a ministerial post in his sights for Ondoa, and works behind the scenes to ensure the Lord's wishes are achieved. Enter stage left the First Lady, who is also keen to see a kindred spirit in the role and thus ensure her influence is felt on the government's HIV/AIDS policy and its use of foreign aid. Lo and behold, within three months of Ondoa taking up her post, she announces that HIV/AIDS can be cured with prayer. Her appointment is a good example of the 7M technique. In an interview with the French journalist Dominic Mesmin, Oyet describes how the 7M ideology is put into practice: "We place Christians in important roles in every sector," he says, and claims that there are at least fifty to a hundred 'born again' Ugandan MPs. "We strategically set them there... we are taking government." The choice of Ondoa, however, doesn't go according to plan. She is unable to keep her ministry under control and in 2013 the president decides to remove her from the post. Ondoa declares it's no surprise because she has already been informed by God to seek another job. She becomes the new Director General of the Uganda Aids Commission.

It would be wrong to suggest all Evangelicals hold the same extreme view and have the goal of discarding all forms of pluralism and individual freedom. But it's certainly true that 'apostles' are exceptionally active worldwide within the charismatic evangelical movement, mixing conservatism with fundamentalism. The result is a significant increase in extremist sentiments being shown within many churches and Christian movements, and the face of Christianity in Africa is slowly but surely changing. Since the new century, it's believed a third of Ugandans have become 'born again' Christians. Peter Wagner now describes the church as a place not for individual salvation, but as the conduit for a transformation to a Christian Utopia in which charismatic Christians take over control of cities and countries from governments.

Pastor Martin Ssempa is the most well-known of the three. His church services on the campus of Makerere University in Kampala attract thousands of people. He understands the art of preaching like no other and makes use of all the modern technology to help him. He's a performer, a man of theatrical gestures, and has learnt how to work an audience as a young break dance champion from East Africa. He grew up without a father, lost a brother and a sister to AIDS, and says that he found God "just in time". Ssempa is close to Janet Museveni, and for a while worked for the American television evangelist Rick Warren of the Saddleback Church in California, another favourite of Uganda's First Lady.

Ssempa often uses objects to illustrate his points. During a television debate with the transgender activist Pepe Onziema, he lays bananas, cucumbers and carrots on the table. They're brought to help him explain lesbian sex. Ssempa is not easy to stop when in full flow and the show's presenter quickly loses control of the discussion. With a breaking voice Ssempa bombards Onziema with 'facts' that suggest a huge amount of fantasy. "I cannot believe you would put me on this show with a hooligan," Onziema says softly to the presenter a little later.

Another example, as reported by *The Observer*, a local Kampala newspaper. It is 18 February 2010. A man is sitting in a deserted auditorium of the Cineplex, a cinema in Kampala, when he receives a text message from a friend: "A sexy film of people doing things is being shown in the Makerere Community Church. It's free." The man immediately realises why he's the only one in the cinema. He springs out of his seat and runs to Martin Ssempa's church. Gay porn is going to be shown. About three hundred people are present. On the podium is a giant screen. It hangs in front of dark blue curtains that run along its entire length. The ventilator in the ceiling helps to cool down the overheated atmosphere in the church. Feelings are already running high. Then the first pictures are shown. Ssempa is adorned in a long, dark toga. As the narrator of the silent film he gives explanations to images that need little clarification. "This is a man licking another man's anus." A man standing next to him on the podium translates his words into the local language. Ssempa's eyes remain focused on the screen. "And this man is eating the poopoo that is now all over his face." He looks across at his audience to gauge the effect his words are having. His index finger remains pointed to the screen. "They start off by touching each other's genitals and smearing each other." A woman in the audience begins to cry and pushes her hands against her ears. A woman sitting in the front is looking at the screen in disgust. She has pulled her young son to her side. Next to her is an old man who's looking around him in astonishment. In Uganda, it's illegal to show pornography. When it's all over one of the audience members complains to *The Observer's* reporter: "Is that the best porn we could get?" He'd hoped to see some lesbian action. Typical for a pastor to show only men. He wants to have a word with him so that, in the future, more 'balanced' films are shown with lesbian and hetero sex. The newspaper reprints the words of one of Ssempa's fellow pastors: "The pastor has shown us a completely new way of luring people to church," he says.

*

Years earlier, at the beginning of the century, the ringleaders of the campaign against homosexuality in Uganda aim their bile at the country's AIDS awareness programme. The spread of the disease is being dramatically reduced, not least due to the campaign to encourage people to use condoms. The Surinamese-Dutch medical doctor Ruben del Prado, working for UNAIDS, is witness to its success. President Museveni, after his election in 1986, quickly takes the initiative, taking action as soon as he realises that many of his soldiers whom he'd lived with in the forests during the freedom struggle have now become infected with HIV. According to a number of sources, it's the Cuban president Fidel Castro who first warns his Ugandan colleague of a pandemic, after Cuban doctors had found the virus in a considerable number of Ugandans who'd been taking part in training exercises in Havana. "My soldiers are going to die," Museveni tells del Prado. "I'm going to beat the drum and the message will be that something has come that is threatening all my people."

Museveni is the first, and for a long time the only African leader, who openly speaks about the need for safe sex, and sets up an ambitious programme focusing on abstinence, monogamy and the use of condoms – the ABC initiative: abstain, be faithful, condomise. The rate of infection drops from the high of eighteen percent at the beginning of the 1990s to just six percent ten years later. But then the First Lady appears on the scene. Del Prado: "She had these beautiful posters distributed with these small birds sitting in a tree, birds with just one partner, such a colourful animal, and the country's national emblem. 'I am a national figure, I am a national bird. I have one partner through life,' was written underneath. For nine months not one single condom was to be found in Uganda. That is just criminal!"

And so the C disappears from the programme. The information booklets are rewritten. Janet Museveni addresses thousands of youngsters and calls on them not to waste their valuable 'airtime' listening to condom propaganda. You get AIDS if you use condoms, is the new message: They have holes in them. The most effective way to avoid the disease is not to have sex – which, of course, cannot be disputed – with monogamy coming a close second. Just like her protégé Martin Ssempa, the First Lady uses inflated rhetoric to get her message across. She compares condom use with theft and murder, and during World AIDS Day in December 2004 she even calls for the number of virgins to be counted, and for that number to be maintained. Her husband completely changes course. Never averse to the military metaphor, he declares in the government's newspaper *New Vision* a war on condom sellers. They're encouraging 'young people into promiscuity' instead of saving lives.

There's such a violent tone to the new policy that organisations that want to continue distributing condoms are afraid they'll be blacklisted and run the risk of having their subsidies removed. In December 2004, the health ministry announces its intention to import fewer condoms. Human Rights Watch points out that the majority of infections occur *within* marriage and describes the decision as "a death sentence for many women". Del Prado watches as posters advocating safe sex and condom use are systematically removed from the streets. Stickers on the backs of buses now read "Born Again". With much fanfare, Martin Ssempa organises the first 'condom burning' event.

Del Prado refuses to be associated with the new policy and speaks out against abstinence as the only form of prevention. "Sex is more than just procreation," he says and, in a last ditch attempt to redress the balance, UNAIDS pays for a glossy poster to be inserted into all newspapers for two days. His willingness to involve local gay groups in the fight against AIDS had already been inflammatory, but the poster is the last straw: his position becomes untenable and the UNAIDS representative in Uganda is called back to head office.

The UN's special representative for HIV/AIDS Stephen Lewis gives an interview with *The New York Times* claiming the new policy in Uganda will be enormously damaging and will lead to an increase in the number of people infected with the virus. He's right. Since 2005, the numbers have started to rise, and the blame can certainly be laid at the door of Uganda's rulers, but Del Prado also sees the hand of the Americans in the unfolding drama. He points to Edward C. Green, an American anthropologist and co-founder of the abstinence AIDS programme of President George W. Bush. Together with Stephen Langa and Martin Ssempa, Green lays down the new policy in a draft document entitled "The Ugandan National Abstinence and Being Faithful Policy on Prevention of Transmission of HIV: Draft Policy and Strategy". Its direct consequence is that all the relevant material relating to HIV in Uganda is rewritten. Accompanying pictures of ejaculation, bodily changes during puberty, and the effectiveness of condoms are no longer permitted. Sex before and outside of marriage is being singled out.

The conservative American influence on the Ugandan AIDS policy starts as soon as Bush becomes president in 2001. Early in his first term, he introduces the President Emergency Plan for Aids Relief – PEPFAR. A budget of fifteen billion dollars is made available to be implemented in developing countries. Bush appoints advisors sceptical of the effectiveness of condom use and adamant upholders of a politics espousing abstinence. Janet Museveni also gets to play her part. Officials from the White House invite her to Washington to tell them how the infection rates in Uganda have fallen, in stark contrast to other African countries. Museveni informs members of Congress that the decrease in the rate, that started a few years earlier as a result of the ABC approach, was now holding firm because of the new information campaigns underlining the message of abstinence before marriage and monogamy. The Bush government decides to reserve a third of the budget for initiatives concentrating solely on these two aspects only. The job of implementing the programmes is handed, in the large part, to religious authorities lacking any real expert knowledge of the AIDS crisis.

The separation of charitable and religious activities is no longer a condition for financial support. Within the White House an employee is given the task of promoting initiatives relating to faith. Bush encourages church groups to become involved. In 2004, around fifteen percent of the fund is being channelled to these particular organisations, but a further speech by the president lets them know "there's a lot more money available".

Rick Warren from the Saddleback Church is present when Bush makes this announcement, and shortly afterwards invites Ugandan pastor Martin Ssempa to his California base to discuss AIDS prevention. The two men get on well. Warren describes Ssempa as his "indispensable sidekick", and his wife says they consider the Ugandan pastor to be like a brother to them. Janet Museveni is not to be upstaged and appears on a giant video screen speaking highly of the religious backed AIDS campaigns taking place in her country. When PEPFAR is evaluated in the American Congress in 2008, the new infection rates are shown to have increased dramatically and the Democrats attempt to remove the conservative elements from the programme. Warren reacts angrily and flies immediately to Washington to take part in a press conference with other right wing Christian leaders. It works. PEPFAR remains unscathed.

Rick Warren is known especially for his promotion of what he calls a "purpose driven life". A book of the same title makes the US bestseller list in 2002. Warren also has his sights set on "purpose driven countries", and has developed his very own 'PEACE' plan, a programme with the grandiose objective of creating a "second Christian reformation". With the help of his wife Kay, he claims his plan is already active in sixty-eight countries. Rwanda is one of them. Its president, Paul Kagame, invites Warren there in 2005. The American attends a number of cabinet meetings and is subsequently given the opportunity to act out his plan in every sector of society. The former Rwandan archbishop Emmanuel Kolini is part of the local committee devoted to implementing Warren's objectives.

He describes homosexuality as a "moral genocide". The comparison is all the more painful considering the recent events in a country where a systematic ethnic slaughter was carried out on a monumental scale.

It's clear in 2005, when Rick Warren holds forth in front of thirty thousand followers in a stadium in California, that 'purpose driven' has little sympathy with the Christian concept of loving one's fellow man. He talks of a 'secret mission' already underway worldwide involving thousands of members of his church. According to him, the teaching of the principles of PEACE are in full swing in four hundred thousand churches, and he predicts a 'revolution', a 'radical expansion of God's kingdom', consciously re-emphasising the word radical: "Only radical people can change the world," he declares. He calls on his followers to do 'whatever it takes'. Great things can be accomplished if they show the same commitment as the disciples of Hitler, Mao and Lenin, he states.

One can take the numbers Warren uses with a large sprinkling of salt, although he also claims to be grossly misunderstood in media reports. No, he has never compared homosexuality with paedophilia and incest. No, he has never actively lobbied against the opening up of marriage for homosexuals in California, even though one just has to look on You Tube to find evidence to the contrary. And no, Peter Wagner from the New Apostolic Reformation was never a mentor, even though his name is on the front page of one of his essays with the term 'mentor' after the comma, clearly visible for all to see. It's Wagner who, in fact, in his speeches, tends to push the rhetoric a little further than Warren. He talks of 'spiritual warfare' and the eventual conquering of state power by the church.

Warren's radicalism and dubious connections have led to a growing criticism in the US. He has subsequently thrown Ssempa overboard. In January 2009, his star rises exponentially when he delivers the invocation prayer at the inauguration of Barack Obama. It puts him into the direct spotlight, leading to more scrutiny of his homophobic pronouncements and his connections with controversial figures. Cracks begin to appear in the prevailing image of a moderate religious leader. Warren needs to respond accordingly and in a video link-up in the same year, he calls on his Ugandan friends to reject the proposed anti-gay law. However, he lends his support to those Anglicans wanting to break from the mother church, claiming to support their views. He calls homosexuality 'unnatural' and the freedom of sexual orientation not a human right.

Warren seems to fit his message according to circumstance, and moderates his tone if public opinion dictates. But he's also not averse to following the line of right wing Christian fundamentalists when the occasion arises, which could be interpreted as an encouragement in the witch-hunt against gays and a license for violence. So is Warren an opportunist? Certainly. Is there method in his actions? Undoubtedly. But it would be an error to squeeze the likes of Warren, Wagner, Ssempa, Lively and Langa into one simple definition. One can be too easily persuaded by reading the analysis of 'kremlinologists' that every new move made by the American Christian right and their African compatriots is somehow part of a grand central plan. The impression is sometimes given that the sheer weight of all the churches and clubs, lobbyists and networks, charities and aid organisations combined will lead inexorably towards a Kingdom of God and a veritable Walhalla of hate. It's fair to say that reporting on the issue tends to overemphasize the victories and underplay the defeats, if the latter gets any coverage at all. There remains the tendency within investigative reporting into the Christian right to play down the characteristic bickering within the Protestant church and the seemingly endless flare-ups between religious scholars. There is little attention paid to the distrust that exists between considerable egos, and to the huge amounts of money involved that has led to some ruthless rivalry. Allegations of plots and conspiracies are often no more than simple panic to a report in the media or the removal of subsidies. The tendency for some reporters to spin interconnecting webs between continents, churches, political agendas and economic interests gives the distorted impression that there is one almighty, unstoppable enemy.

But there are times when eye-catching associations do come to light, and show that the agenda of the Christian right isn't only about inciting homophobia or meddling with information campaigns over AIDS, and the fight against the right to abortion. In 2012, a short YouTube film appears about the Ugandan warlord Joseph Kony who, since the 1990s, has been the commander of the Lord's Resistance Army (LRA) and has been responsible for large-scale atrocities in the north of the country. The documentary is called *Kony*

2012 and is made by the American non-profit organisation Invisible Children. It creates a media sensation and the film goes viral. In the wake of all the publicity, the makers of the film also come under close scrutiny, and investigations show links between the financers of the film, religious fundamentalism, oil interests and the arms trade.

Lira is a small city in northern Uganda and the site of one of the LRA's worst atrocities. Invisible Children decides to show *Kony 2012* there, and erects a giant screen in Mayor's Garden, the city park. Thousands turn up to watch. It's already been viewed by tens of millions of people around the world. Now it's their turn. They come from all around, walking and cycling to the park. They've heard the film promises to tell their story: how over the previous twenty years, Kony has murdered and destroyed families, kidnapped children and made them soldiers in his LRA, and how, since 2006, the region has been picking up the pieces following the Ugandan army's successful push to hunt Kony out of the country's territory. But things don't quite go as expected. When it's over, there's an angry shout from someone in the audience: "This has nothing to do with us!" What they'd watched is a film containing predominantly white Americans. Why are filmmaker Jason Russell and Invisible Children, the organisation he co-founded, the main focus of the film instead of the victims themselves? Why are all these Americans walking around in t-shirts with the picture or name of the hated Kony on it? "What would they think if we went around wearing a t-shirt with the head of Osama bin Laden on it?" asks one angry woman. The screening ends in chaos. Stones are thrown at the screen.

The documentary reveals very little about the background to the conflict and, as a consequence, much of the context is lost. President Museveni is presented through rose tinted glasses – north Uganda's population know only too well his soldiers are also guilty of war crimes. And then comes salvation in the form of American military action aimed at arresting Kony, something the filmmakers are calling for. There's just a throw away remark that Kony has already withdrawn from the territory and is now confined to operating in the neighbouring countries South Sudan, Congo and the Central African Republic.

The filmmakers use footage that is almost ten years old and sketch a conflict that is factually out-dated and one-sided. As early as 2005, Human Rights Watch asks the International Criminal Court in The Hague to look into atrocities carried out by *both* sides, the LRA and the Ugandan army. But it now seems that an elite American unit can solve all the problems by rushing in and arresting Kony. In the weeks before the screening in Mayor's park, Invisible Children distributes thousands of action packets containing, among other things, a poster and t-shirt. Worldwide, a massively successful publicity campaign is launched using graffiti stickers. There is some criticism here and there, but it's shouted down by the noise of a campaign in which 'we', the West, are able to finally bring some order to a country that has already experienced so much torment.

The massive interest in the documentary leads to further scrutiny of Invisible Children's own history. It's found to have a bank account in the Cayman Islands, not the obvious choice for a non-profit making organisation. But even more remarkable are the connections Russell appears to have with Christian fundamentalist groups in the US. A clip can be seen on the internet of him speaking at Liberty University at the end of 2011, and as with so many other organisations in this environment, it's worth delving a little further to see who's behind it. Until recently, the dean of the university's law school is Mat Staver, the founder of the Liberty Counsel and a vocal supporter of Uganda's anti-gay law. He's also part of Scott Lively's legal team following a case brought against him in March 2012 by Ugandan gay activists and the Centre for Constitutional Rights, for inciting hatred. The complaint is judged admissible in August 2014 by Michael Ponsor, a district judge in Springfield, Massachusetts, which could lead to a conviction for crimes against humanity. It's the investigative journalist Bruce Wilson who discovers that Invisible Children is bankrolled by some of America's biggest Christian fundamentalist organisations, including the National Christian Foundation, described as "the largest donor of the hard-line, anti-homosexual, creationist Christian right". It appears that the very same religious groups that have been financing the anti-gay campaigns in Uganda are also the sponsors of *Kony 2012*.

There is now considerable international coverage of the role that American fundamentalists are playing in the fight against equal rights for LGBT people in Africa. For many years, gay activists have let no opportunity escape in making the connection between discriminatory laws in many African countries and their British-Victorian origins, but the more recent stories circulating about the influence of the likes of Lively and Warren have led to a shift in the blame. It does little justice to the impact and enthusiasm of local anti-gay activists such as Ssempa and Bahati. These men and their supporters are being all too easily painted as executors of a foreign agenda. The reasoning of many African LGBT activists can be compared with those who claim the movement for equal rights is being driven and encouraged by outside forces. Those who lay the blame for the anti-gay campaigns solely at the door of the American Christian right buy directly into the myth of a once pure and unblemished Africa, a paradise on earth, spoilt by the malign influence of everyone from Western and Arabic slave drivers, to colonial rulers and the Protestant architects of Apartheid. The shrewdness with which many African politicians carry out their functions seems not to be taken too seriously, but one just has to look a little inquiringly into the performances of Yoweri Museveni on the East Middle Africa stage to see a deeply experienced strategist at work. The end justifies the means – in all its Machiavellian insight.

Museveni is very aware of how important his country has become for the American religious lobbies. These groups see Uganda as the frontline against the advancing tide of Islam. Neighbouring countries such as Kenya and Tanzania have a mixed religious population, whereas Islam has gained little foothold in

Uganda. But the Americans have been interested in the country ever since the slaughter of Christians in the 1970s under its former dictator Idi Amin. Not long after his election victory in 1986, Museveni received a visit from a member of 'The Family', a Christian fundamentalist US-based network. A book about the network, written by Jeff Sharlet, describes it as an elite group that has its sights set on the "powerful key men chosen by God to direct affairs of the nation". Free market ideology and God's word are effortlessly interwoven. The Family is a "Christian-capitalist group with a neo-colonial vision of the world" according to Sharlet, and within the network itself it's known as a 'Christian Mafia' due to its secretive operations. Its members show their face just once a year, at the National Prayer Breakfast, a massive prayer service graced by the presence of the US President. The fact that The Family makes overtures with Museveni shortly after his election victory is based on the assessment that he will become 'the key man in Africa' for fundamentalist lobbies and Washington's leaders – a strategic ally during the Cold War and against Islam.

In the following years, David Bahati and James Nsaba Buturo (who for a while holds the post of Uganda's minister of Ethics and Integrity) both become members of The Family. The middleman between the network and Museveni (as well as other African leaders) is the Republican senator Jim Inhofe. The co-operation brings evangelicalism ever closer to a number of important contemporary issues in Africa – the campaign against homosexuality, the access to Africa's mineral wealth, and the forming of geopolitical alliances.

Inhofe is known within the US senate as a mouthpiece for the oil industry. Concerns about the climate are dismissed as part of a 'liberal agenda'. He's also a fervent supporter of an American military presence in Africa and is on record as expressing his delight that there is absolutely no sign of homosexuality being present in his family. He considers himself an Africa expert, not least due to the 132 times he's visited the continent. It's a little odd then that, during an interview on *The Rachel Maddow Show* in 2012, a popular programme in the US, he denies any knowledge of the anti-gay bill in Uganda and of any acquaintance with David Bahati.

The discovery of vast oil fields in 2006 gives an extra dimension to Uganda's attraction. Lake Albert, which stretches over the borders of both Uganda and the DRC, is expected to produce 200 thousand barrels of crude oil every day. The extraction is due to start in 2017, with three oil companies given the go-ahead to work there: the British Tullow Oil, the French Total, and the Chinese CNOOC. If the proceeds are used to benefit the local population, it could lead to Uganda being removed from the list of low-income countries. The oil discovery has also led to speculation that Museveni might be tempted to increase his military might in the region. China's rise on the African stage has also given the Americans food for thought and the added incentive to do more to protect their interests, especially in Central Africa.

The hunt for Kony can also be seen as part of that strategy. One of the most powerful voices behind the calls for his capture is the 'oil man' Jim Inhofe, who also happens to be a member of the Senate Armed Forces Committee and can be seen a number of times in *Kony 2012* calling for a military 'solution' to the problem. In May 2009, he puts his weight behind a law obliging the US to provide military assistance to the governments of Uganda and neighbouring countries with the aim of disarming the LRA and protecting civilians. This law is still pending when operation Lightening Thunder is launched in the DRC in December 2009 to rout the LRA. Uganda, Congo and South Sudan all take part, with the support of the Americans. It's a total failure. Kony escapes and his soldiers kill hundreds of civilians in retaliation. Despite this, President Obama still signs the bill into law. Invisible Children describes the President's signature as a major victory and boasts that it's a direct result of its own lobbying work. A year or so later, more 'special forces' are sent to Uganda. Again the mission fails.

Why does the US send soldiers to the middle of Africa to advise the Ugandan army on how to apprehend or kill one man, political analysts ask themselves? Kony is no threat to US national security, has for many years been successfully hiding in an area the size of France, and his army is a fraction of the size it once was. The most commonly heard reply to the question is that it's a reward for Uganda's role, as part of the peace-keeping force of the African Union, in the fight against Al-Shabaab in Somalia. The growing threat of Islamic terrorism in parts of Africa is seen as a 'national security risk' for the US. This is also evident in senator Inhofe's reaction to the terror attack in the country's capital Kampala on 11 July 2010. Seventy-four people are killed following suicide bombings on crowds watching the final of the football World Cup. An American employee of Invisible Children is among the victims. Inhofe again emphasizes the importance of an American military strategy to work together with African states in order to defeat terrorism. The impression is that Kony is the excuse needed to deploy more American military advisors in the region.

The over-simplistic message in *Kony 2012* is a big PR success for Museveni. He's not only represented as a man determined to root out evil, but also gains support for his military strategy in the region. It's known that some of the employees of Invisible Children are giving direct support to the Ugandan secret service. Documents from the American embassy, published by Wikileaks, show that in 2009 Invisible Children tip the Ugandans off when the former child soldier Patrick Komakech shows up. The organisation has good contacts with him. In one of its videos, Komakech describes how he was kidnapped by rebels at the age of nine. Museveni's troops react immediately to the new information and Komakech is arrested. During the 'interrogation' — according to human rights groups, torture is a routine practice — the young man confesses to being part of a 'new movement' that is 'intent on overthrowing the government'. Komakech gives them names. There's a new wave of arrests. Many claim their innocence. Leaked documents show that the Ugandan government then deliberately makes false allegations against a number of its critics. The Catholic bishop John Baptist Odama, a prominent opponent of Museveni's military adventures, is accused of lending his support to Kony's LRA and being a member of this 'new movement'.

In December 2013, under pressure from Inhofe, the US announces that it will add an extra fifty million dollars for 'logistical assistance' in the Ugandan army's hunt for Kony. A few months later, President Obama decides to send military planes and another hundred and fifty of his 'special forces'. Caitlin Hayden, the spokesperson for the US National Security Council, says the planes and helicopters will be stationed in Uganda so they can be deployed when necessary in the Central African Republic, the DRC, and South Sudan. The duration of the deployment is not clear. The US military presence in the region is growing and is clearly not exclusively for the hunt for Kony. Access to raw materials is also an issue, together with the strengthening of ties in the war on terror. This must all be taken into account when assessing America's carefully worded approach to Uganda's anti-gay campaigns.

Museveni has good reason not to jeopardise relations with the US. As the main 'warmonger' in the region, he must utilise his alliance with the US to best advantage. He had access to massive untapped natural resources in neighbouring Congo as a consequence of Uganda's active participation in the 1990s war there, and according to the investigative journalist Angelo Izama, in 2000 Uganda exported eleven tonnes of gold whilst only producing 0.00441 tonnes. The massive oil reserves in South Sudan, the third largest oil producer in Africa, is clearly a major factor in Uganda's involvement there, despite the rhetoric of 'bringing stability', 'preventing Kony from establishing a base there', and 'evacuating Ugandan nationals'. All worthy aims, but ultimately Museveni has his eyes set on a share of the oil revenues.

But it's not just about natural resources. Military campaigns, just as those against homosexuality, draw attention away from poverty, corruption and AIDS. They also assure Museveni of the military's continuing support. Conflicts and perceived threats also give legitimacy to new repressive laws aimed at curtailing freedom of speech and the freedom to associate. There have even been times when Museveni has been able to position himself as peacemaker, even when it's been him who's stoked the conflict.

Museveni is a master of political manoeuvring and is adept at playing off friends and enemies alike, whether it's within his own party or the international community. Comparisons can be made with Robert Mugabe, but Museveni is more accomplished in the art of saying the right thing at the right time, even if the message contradicts his previous statements. He thus manages to remain on friendly terms with almost everyone: Americans, Russians, Chinese, and yes, even some representatives of Uganda's gay movement have been lured into believing they can trust their president. When he signs the anti-gay law to win over opponents within his party, then it's "all in the game". The Constitutional Court overturns the decision – Museveni doesn't flinch. That also serves a purpose.

Chapter 7

"Sodo-Miites"

A glimmer of pink light is appearing on Africa's horizon. Which of Africa's (former) rulers are speaking out for tolerance and equal rights? Gays and lesbians have entered the novels of today's African writers. There are the first 'pink soaps' coming out of Nollywood, and LGBT photographers and artists get international recognition.

'Coming out' stories in literature are ten to the dozen and tend towards a familiar pattern. The protagonist has been wrestling for many years with 'strange' feelings. There's nobody they can talk to. Out of a fear of rejection they recoil from the world. Thoughts of suicide enter their head – an end to all this misery. And then comes an act of great courage spurred on by a specific encounter. The moment of catharsis has arrived. Finally, the words come out. *I am* . . . and so on! More often than not, reactions from family and friends are positive. There's understanding and acceptance. "I've always had a suspicion," some will say. But however hackneyed these stories may be, they still have the power to move.

On occasion, a 'coming out' story will catch the public's imagination. It's generally involving someone with celebrity status, although it's even more newsworthy if a sports personality or a government minister is involved. The headlines follow a certain trajectory. First the 'breaking news', followed by how courageous people think it is, even though some had their suspicions all along. But isn't all this a touch odd when, in this modern world, to be who you are and say what you want is considered a person's right? And yet there's still a tacit obligation to have to declare one's sexual preference (of the gay kind). The debate rages on and, in the meantime, you become the 'role model' – a sought after guest on talk shows and a keynote speaker at Gay Pride.

If there's one African who personifies and, without a doubt, embellishes the 'coming out' story, then it has to be the Kenyan writer Binyavanga Wainaina, known as 'the Binj' to his friends. Wainaina is enjoying a growing reputation, not only in Kenya but on the African continent and beyond. He first comes to fame in 2002 when his short story, *Discovering Home,* wins the prestigious Caine Prize for African literature. His controversial essay *How to write about Africa,* which appears in the British literary magazine *Granta* three years later, attracts a lot more attention. The essay is an ironic dissection of clichés and preconceptions about Africa:

"Always use the word Africa or darkness or safari in your title . . . in your text, treat Africa as if it were one country. It is hot and dusty with rolling grasslands and huge herds of animals and tall, thin people who are starving . . . Let them dance!"

He also founds the writer's collective *Kwani?* in Nairobi, a bevy of 'angry young (wo)men' and a hotbed of literary talent and free thinkers. In 2007, when unrest grips parts of the country after a disputed general election, he sends an email to the hundred or so members of his collective with just one word attached – write! The eruption of ethnic tensions and violence, that culminates with a number of Kenyans being brought before the International Criminal Court in The Hague, is the catalyst for the emergence of a striking number of short stories, poems and other writing sharing an antipathy towards a self-important ruling elite not averse to inciting violence if its interests are at stake.

A few years ago, we were present at readings Wainaina gave from his own body of work during the biannual *Kwani? Litfest* in a crowded nightspot in the centre of Nairobi. Poetry mixed effortlessly with disco lights. It's no wonder the World Economic Forum in Davos nominates the Binj as a 'young global leader', and that in 2010 he's the recipient of a Prince Claus Prize – one of the Netherland's most prestigious awards.

On 19 January 2014, Wainaina publishes a brief text on three separate blogs – in Nairobi, Cape Town, and New York. The title is: *I am a homosexual, mum*. It's presented as a 'missing chapter' from a piece published three years earlier entitled *One day I will write about this place*. It starts with a "fictional version of events" during the time of his mother's death in 2000 from the effects of diabetes. Wainaina rushes back to Nairobi from South Africa, where he's studying, holds her hand as she lies on her death bed, and whispers into her ear: "I am a homosexual, mum."

The truth, however, is quite different. In reality, he's unable to get a visa in time – leaving South Africa quickly and without the relevant documentation could result in him being refused re-entry and unable to finish his studies. Wainaina's story then continues with childhood memories of his father who dies a little over ten years after his mother:

"*I am five years old. He stood there, in overalls, awkward, his chest a railway track of sweaty bumps, and little hard beads of hair. Everything about him is smooth-slow. Bits of brown on a cracked tooth, that endless long smile . . . he lifts me in the air and swings. He smells of diesel, and the world of all other people's movements has disappeared . . . there are no creaks in him, like a tractor he will climb any hill, steadily. If he walks away, now, with me, I will go with him forever. I know if he puts me down my legs will not move again. I am so ashamed, I stop myself from clinging. I jump away from him and avoid him forever. For twentysomething years, I even hug men awkwardly.*"

The feelings released from the touch of his father keep returning:

"*Stronger, firmer now. Aged maybe seven. Once with another slow easy golfer at Nakuru Golf Club, and I am shaking because he shook my hand. Then I am crying alone in the toilet because the repeat of this feeling has made me suddenly ripped apart and lonely. The feeling is not sexual. It is certain. It is overwhelming. It wants to make a home. It comes every few months like a bout of malaria and leaves me shaken for days, and confused for months. I do nothing about it."*

Many years later, on a visit to London, Wainaina has his first brief homosexual encounter, but keeps the experience to himself. He thinks his friends probably suspect something (and after his coming out, a Kenyan newspaper writes that Nairobi has been awash with rumours for years) but Wainaina remains silent. Until this day in January 2014.

It's not just the imaginative power of Wainaina's writing and the deceptively simple way he manages to express what it's like to be homosexual that gives such depth and originality to his work, it's also the sincerity and honesty – a heartfelt cry of literary verve that gives an extraordinary energy to his creations. But, Wainina says, it's a heart that he never allowed to grow: "I touch no men. I read books." Now that his secret is out, wrapped in a love paean to his parents, he writes, "My heart is learning to stretch." He's finally told them what he was unable to do during their lifetime. "I have never thrown my heart at you mum. You have never asked me to." And why? "I did not trust you," he writes apologetically.

There's a massive public reaction to Wainaina's literary disclosure. The internet response is overwhelming and supportive, with a stream of likes and shares. Others tell their own 'coming out' stories. It remains Nairobi's main topic of conversation for days to come, and just twenty-four hours after the 'lost chapter' appears, a surprise party is organised by friends and family in honour of Wainaina's birthday and 'for coming out of the closet'. The international media follows. Newspapers, radio and television stations from all over the world report on the writer's public affirmation.

What accounts for all this attention, nationally and internationally? Of course, the beauty and originality of his writing plays a large role. If an Oscar existed for 'best coming out story', then Wainaina would have been a shoe-in for the 2014 award. But the timing is also a factor. For many weeks beforehand, there had been a series of negative images coming out of Africa relating to homosexuality: an angry crowd advances towards the office of an LGBT club in the Ivory Coast and arrests are made; there's further tightening of anti-gay laws in Nigeria and Uganda. Wainaina had been highly vocal on these issues for some time, using social media to share his views. A few months before publishing the 'lost chapter', he takes part in a debate about the decision to place the novel *The Whale Rider*, by the known gay New Zealand writer Witi Ihimaera, on the set reading list for Kenyan high schools. "A child growing up in this country will meet a homosexual, but you can't maintain purity by shutting out everything you don't agree with. This is part of ancient madness," Wainaina says in his response to calls for its censorship. And when, in the same period, the Kenyan newspaper the *Daily Nation* asks him why, at the age of forty-two, he hasn't yet married, he replies: "Because I haven't yet found a reason to."

Wainaina's announcement doesn't just trigger messages of support. "What's the big deal?" a fellow blogger asks. "You're gay, I'm hetero, what does it matter?" Another blog waspishly suggests it's a great new way of attracting attention. And, of course, the customary accusations appear in the Kenyan media. How is Wainaina going to answer to God? Is it surprising that he has been lured to commit a homosexual act in far-away London (although Wainaina states that it was his initiative)? Does he not understand anything about the 'African culture'? Wainaina is playing directly into the hands of Western imperialists. "It is Adam and Eve, not Adam and *Steve*! How can the earth go on if there are no more children being born? It's immoral." The *Daily Nation* journalist Kwamchetsi Makokha adds his penny's worth with a wonderful display of ironic humour:

"For an African man of his unique talents and numerous achievements, Binyavanga should know better than to go revealing the continent's secrets to the world. Africans have never been gay, at least not publicly. They cannot start now. That is why, as an African, Binyavanga must uphold, promote and protect the doctrine of heterosexuality according to the natural order . . . The mere thought of same-sex relations irks African gods so much that they visit drought, locusts and pestilence upon the continent . . . In South Africa, vigilantes against gay activity administer corrective rape on lesbians; in Uganda and Nigeria, they make strict laws to formally save gay people from angry mobs that would lynch them."

Makokha's article receives a huge response from the newspaper's readership, the majority not fully realising its sardonic pitch. "You are 150% correct. Tell them again! I am just fed up about everything Western being shoved down our throats in the name of human rights." Although one reader writes that Makokha shouldn't exaggerate: "Gays shouldn't be blamed for *all* the continent's natural disasters, otherwise those who oppose homosexuality may once again have cause to doubt."

The way in which Wainaina's 'coming out' is the precursor to a 'free for all' for so many people to express an opinion will have come as no surprise to the writer. The issue is too important to him for it to be taken lightly or flippantly, and there's every reason to believe he was busy anticipating the fallout even before his piece was published. Just days after it appears, he uploads six short testimonies to YouTube. They're viewed thousands of times by friend and foe alike. The first is an explanation of why Wainaina decided to make this open declaration. The catalyst, he says, was the death of a young gay friend called Kalota. The man's sexual identity was completely suppressed at the funeral service, replaced by disparaging and cryptic remarks from many of those present. Kalota's parents were later forced to leave their church as a consequence of their son's sexuality, and local church leaders were conspicuously absent from the private memorial service later organised by The Binj and other friends. He describes this small tragedy as symptomatic of a society that has destroyed the imagination. For years, Kenya has been a one party state with one prevailing opinion and an obedient media (it was only in 2002 that Daniel Arap Moi relinquished the dictatorship, after twenty-five years in power). The education curriculum of the former British rulers was kept on, just as in many other postcolonial countries in Africa. Wainaina:

"What you have is the same school that said, 'Bring the obedient children of you Africans to this school so that you can become clerks. And then we drum a syllabus into you, make you go sing "God Save the Queen"'... the syllabus of I don't know what you call: moral-boring, moral-flat, moral-crap. It's horrible! ... How do you have an educational system that makes us think and innovate? Why do I feel like I've gone places where you sit with a bunch of kids and they challenge you in class, and here, to challenge a thing in class is to be bringing, as my maths teacher used to call it, queer behaviour."

There's a mentality in Kenya that believes in the concept of demons, he says, and it happens in environments where there's no public discussion, and where education and growing up is all about drilling the mentality of slavish obedience into you. It's drummed into you by pastors and preachers – the 'brokers of the forces'. Is something wrong? Then it's because someone is messing with you – it must be because demons are present in the neighbour. Those who remove their demons will prosper. The pastors, according to Wainaina, will say, "I've been given power because I went to Nigeria for Bible study, and I've been taught how to handle these forces." He then gives another example of their 'mind-numbing' practices:

"Mum took me to a funeral of a guy — let's call the guy Paul. Paul was much older than me, and he had a

tragic story about him, when I was a kid: he was sixteen, and he had taken the car, and then he knocked a kid and the kid died. So now Paul is knocked back — hit-and-run . . . Nobody really knows this story, because he was found dead . . . So we go for a funeral. First, the whole angle of the testimony was: 'We really don't know if in that microsecond, before that car hit him, he confessed his sins and then he's gone to heaven. But I must tell you that if he did not, he's burning in hell right now.' And there are the parents clapping in this ecstasy of madness."

Wainaina says he has counted twenty-seven churches in the neighbourhood where he grew up:

"The way the churches are built is so nice. Poor people paid to build churches that are beautiful and expensive. But the places you are supposed to build for your children's imagination to grow to build new things, I don't see them."

The significance of Wainaina's narrative lies especially in the fact that he's not in the least tempted to become involved in the generalisations that so often dominate the debate on homosexuality. He couldn't care less if people conclude that it doesn't fit in with African culture, or doesn't respect traditions or faith, or claim that it's a 'western product'. All of these, he argues, stem from a lack of imagination, and many Africans are still thinking within the boundaries set by the *mzungu* (whites). The way many of his countrymen pronounce the word sodomite (which he describes as 'the most Victorian word *ever*) is a typical example. 'Sodo-Miites' Wainaina exclaims - with a prolonged emphasis of the third syllable and a theatrical roll of the final 's', as though, when you say it, 'the world is supposed to shake'. He also swipes aside the plea to return to the 'values of the original African society':

"Give me data that says that the people who speak three thousand languages in this continent — you have communities of twenty-five million — who belong to one kingdom . . . So what's an African society? At least do the data."

The accusation that traditional marriage is threatened if gays are permitted to tie the knot is also rejected:

"I'm not interested in gay marriage. If that thing comes three generations from now, that is cool . . . Already there are four states in Nigeria where you're going to be stoned to death by law if you're even suspected of [homosexuality]. That's Sharia law. That's like shit-from-a-thousand-years-ago hate."

He calls it a witch-hunt.

But with what does Wainaina want to replace all this hate and suspicion?

"I believe that Africa is rising. There's a kind of a spirit, a level of creativity, that's growing, and that creativity itself is always under risk from the Puritans. Now, I'm not interested in saying that the Puritans must go away. Everybody has Puritans. In a family it's always nice to have one or two. In a society it's always nice to have many. It's okay. I'm an African, I was brought up here, my home is here (...) Being an Afropolitan, I am here to stay. I want to live inside an ecosystem where people go and say not that there's a demon next door but 'There's a thing I don't understand next door, and I don't have to understand it. Because that person's right to be a demon the way they want is theirs. And me, I have mine. And if my values are strong, I don't need to go running to beat, arrest, or peep inside people's bedrooms.'"

Of course Wainaina is African. More still, Pan-African, but he refuses to declare his religious beliefs, or which parts of Africa's traditions he holds dear, although he laughs at the idea that homosexuality is 'un-African'. His dream is to establish an African refuge, where people feel safe and free. He's set it in motion by blasting his way out of the closet, by posting a constant stream of messages on social media, and with his unerring ability to think out of the box. The Facebook message that he was to become the new Kenyan ambassador to Uganda was also widely shared and 'liked'. Alas, it was an April Fool's joke.

The depressing picture that Wainaina portrays of Kenya and Africa is something open to question. The writer himself is a proponent of how a new generation of free thinkers are changing the intellectual landscape – a post-postcolonial generation who are treading outside conventional boundaries set by the former oppressors *and* the leaders who took over the reins of power after independence. This new generation has created the likes of *Kwani?* in Nairobi and *Chimurenga* in Cape Town, as well as writers from the highly popular *Africa is a Country* blog – all breeding grounds for troublemakers and unruly creative souls. They're undoubtedly the driving force behind a new, distinctive, powerful voice that can be heard day in, day out in the African blogosphere, and at literary festivals, and debating clubs in schools and universities. They make their presence known wherever possible – reacting to controversial statements in online newspapers, writing divisive rants on social media, and often taking part in radio phone-in shows. These windows of opportunity are increasing, with the topic of homosexuality a perennial hot topic. Of course, there are still many obedient, uncritical journalistic publications – where aren't? – but what is particularly striking is the rapid growth of independent media on the continent. Many of Africa's newspapers still toe the government line, but divergent opinions are now being given space and airtime. When defining the media, one must take care not to attribute the mouthpieces of Africa's ruling elite with one uniform anti-gay voice. It's known that within these elites there is disagreement and heated discussion. One of *Behind the Mask's* correspondents in Zimbabwe also worked for *The Herald*, the newspaper of President Mugabe's ruling ZANU-PF party.

Equally remarkable is the fact that there's a debate going on in a number of African countries between traditional leaders. Most, of course, speak adamantly against any relaxation of laws when the subject is raised, but just as noteworthy is the way in which many African gay activists are striking back. A notable example is the workshop organised by the Botswana based human rights group BONELA in July 2013. In front of twenty-five *dikgosi* (tribal elders), an employee of the organisation talks about his gay experiences in Botswana:

"After counselling and advice from my doctor I came to the conclusion that I could not be treated for it. I took my sister into my confidence and told her that I was gay. Her answer: 'ke sale ke go bone' (I could have told you that myself). My mother's reaction was one of shock. She hadn't any idea. She implored me to find a cure but until now nothing's come of it. My brother was very unpleasant

about it all, called me a disgrace to the family and said that I was possessed by demons. He made me very unhappy and I thought about killing myself."

The *dikgosi* reacts sympathetically to the man's testimony. There have always been gays here, one of them explains. Another says there's even a word for it in the country's original language – *mantanyola*. There's then a discussion over whether homosexuality is at odds with African culture or the teachings of the Bible. The first is not difficult to answer – "No culture forbids homosexuality," one of them says. But is it at odds with the Bible? That's possible. "But the Bible is against things that we now find quite normal, such as equal rights for women," one says. "Or polygamy," says another. They all see the law as being above tradition, and cite the well-known Botswanan former High Court judge Unity Dow who says that religious and cultural beliefs tend to be patriarchal in character, but the law is not, and it's the law that must be observed.

Once the workshop is over, the gay man tells a journalist from *Mmegi*, a Botswanan newspaper, that he's relieved the elders reacted so positively to what he had to say. "I could see in their faces that they were moved by my story. They showed a lot of understanding and wanted to know more. One of them suggested that there should be a follow up workshop in which a lesbian is invited to talk."

With the conspicuous rise of the African activist, as well as their defenders, another of the West's preconceived ideas can be jettisoned. The former Archbishop Desmond Tutu is not the only senior figure within Africa's Anglican community who speaks out for equal rights, and South Africa is not the only country on the continent where support for this principle can be found. In June 2011, Willy Mutunga, a firm supporter of equal rights, is named as Kenya's chief justice. At the turn of the century, Zambia's first president Kenneth Kaunda speaks out against the persecution of homosexuals. His comments are followed a few years later by Botswana's former president Festus Mogae. In a debate on the BBC, he is asked why he hadn't spoken up earlier when he was still the country's president. "I wanted to win the election," he answers honestly. In March 2016, the Botswana Court of Appeals allows LGBT organisations to register and campaign for changes in legislation. Mozambique's former president Joachim Chissano, Mogae's colleague, comes out in favour of equal rights in 2014, almost a decade after leaving office. Joyce Banda, however, is more forthright, and not long after being sworn in as Malawi's fourth president, declares homosexuals will no longer be prosecuted. In September 2013, the new prime minister of Senegal Aminata Touré raises high hopes amongst LGBT activists when she appoints a justice minister well-known as a supporter of equal rights. A couple of months later, Zambia's then first lady, the gynaecologist Dr Christine Kaseba-Sata, calls for an open discussion on 'men who have sex with other men' and, in a speech to workers from UN-AIDS, says they shouldn't be discriminated against on the grounds of their sexual preference. It receives an enthusiastic welcome. Her words are described as 'astonishing': "Its importance cannot be overstated." Some gay activists see it differently and point to Kaseba-Sata's emphasis on the risk of HIV infection that women run when their men sleep with other men. It's tantamount to her declaring homosexuality should be treated as an illness, they say; something the World Health Organisation distanced itself from in 1990. The *Lusaka Times* also takes the same line: "Homosexuality threatens to undo the fight against AIDS" is its headline. However, it's clear that the First Lady's call for the issue to be discussed is a major step forward. After all, why talk about something that many Zambians claim doesn't even exist within its borders?

And in June 2015, Mozambique announces that homosexuality will be decriminalised.

Pleas for greater understanding, tolerance and equal rights aren't just coming from one specific, eloquent corner of a modern, radical Africa, such as the writer's collectives in Nairobi and Cape Town. Political, religious and tribal leaders are also speaking out, lawyers are becoming more vocal as advocates for freedom and constitutional reform, and there are clear divisions appearing within regional organisations such as the African Union (AU) and the South African Development Community (SADC), where it's no longer South Africa against the rest. In April 2015, the African Commission on Human Rights (an advisory commission of the AU) awards official observer status to the Coalition for African Lesbians. Just as noteworthy is the publication of so-called 'peer reviews' by the AU (member states are judged by each other on issues such as human rights, social justice, etc.) in which the South African police is heavily criticised for its inability to stop violence against lesbians. South African activists, for their part, are calling for their country to take a more assertive role within international organisations, and accuse government representatives of being too circumspect. One diplomat, off the record, says they have to be cautious: "We're sometimes accused of having imperialist leanings, with a tendency to lecture the rest of Africa." Another declares it's important not to jeopardise economic interests, although according to one Cape Town gay activist "some are out and out homophobes". But praise must be given where praise is due: South African representatives to the UN are applauded for their role in persuading a number of fellow African countries not to vote against a resolution put forward by Brazil calling for an end to discrimination based on sexual orientation (most abstain). There's also recognition for the South African lawyer Navi Pillay, the UN High Commissioner for Human Rights until mid-2014, who speaks out in no uncertain terms against discrimination of LGBT people.

One of the results of the debate that's been raging in Africa for the past twenty years is that the argument homosexuality doesn't exist on the continent no longer holds water. So often did we hear these claims during our travels through African countries? "No, really, seriously, I've never seen it," one said. "Gays here? You're joking, right?" says another. Of course, it's not difficult to miss wasn't it also habitually hidden from view, but sometimes it's a question of closing your eyes to what's in front of your nose? It could also be that there are different perceptions of what homosexuality means in practice and how homosexuals are supposed to behave. Two men walking hand in hand will not necessarily be construed as anything other than friendship (which is often true), and earrings are not considered an expression of a gay identity – although in 1998, when the Ugandan president Yoweri Museveni calls on people to report homosexuals, Christopher, a gay doctor, is immediately telephoned by family members: "Take out your earrings! They're looking for you!"

During the research for this book and conversations with people from all walks of life, it became clear that even amongst arch-conservative church leaders there's an acknowledgement 'they' do exist. It might be said grudgingly and through gritted teeth, with a total lack of enthusiasm, and with the caveat that these are lost souls who must be restored to the right path, but the recognition of the existence of homosexuality in their midst is there all the same. How can it be otherwise, when even a journalist from Uganda's main news programme is neutrally reporting a legal victory for a local gay movement, surrounded by dozens of celebrating LGBT activists on the terrace of the Speke Hotel in the centre of Kampala!

But all things considered, it would be a gross misnomer to suggest that Africa's English-speaking garden is full of flowers in bud, waiting to bloom. Yes, there have been encouraging signs for those advocating equal rights, but zooming in a little closer, one discovers many, often contradictory, tendencies. It's easy to paint a stereotypical picture of a continent moving forward. But when we try to put the case for a rosier future during discussions with gay activists, they hit back by talking about the tightening of laws against them, intimidation, prosecution, abuse, rape, and leaders with a homophobic agenda. It's difficult to respond positively to such overwhelming evidence, but one can also suggest that these setbacks can be seen as a reaction to the positive changes taking place in many African countries; not that such sentiments can soften the pain caused to the victims of homophobic violence.

The tendency of many to squeeze Africa into one simple, generic box is nothing new. *The* Africans think this, *the* Africans think that. It leaves little room for the many shades of grey that lie between. The unrest sown by African demagogues only helps to intensify the image that all is not well there, whilst the statistics showing economic growth over the past ten years is feeding the opposite stereotype – that it's all hunky-dory. Hyperbole flourishes. When it all went belly-up in Africa, postcolonial leaders were rudderless, civil wars ravaged the continent, and it was all sickness and hunger. In 1994, the famous American journalist Robert Kaplan prophesised an impending Armageddon in the article *The Coming Anarchy* published in *The Atlantic Monthly*. Africa will be carved up by warlords and become the epicentre of civil war and failed states. At the turn of the century, the front page of *The Economist* reads "Africa, Hopeless Continent". Its opinion has vacillated ever since. In 2013, the same magazine's lead story is "Africa Rising": the Asian miracle is coming to Africa, and from Addis Ababa to Lagos, a rapidly growing middle class is making their way to new shopping malls and beauty parlours. Good times, bad times. It's Africa as soap opera.

Every era tends to have one pervading narrative that gnaws away at a more complex truth. Western 'Afroholics' will argue until they're blue in the face that, even during the bad times, Africa was a paradise on earth. Yes, the people were poor, but solidarity and community spirit pulled them through – laughing and dancing and always welcoming. Why? That's simple. *We* have the clock and *they* have the time – a paradise of calm and space. Now the 'golden century' seems to have arrived, full of impressive statistics of economic growth and a middle class sweeping across Africa's savanna, romantics claim. But if you take any notice of the international do-gooders' press releases, then 'indigenous peoples' are being swept away; international terrorism has its sights firmly set on the African continent; and the ubiquitous slums are a ticking time bomb that can explode at any moment. And you realize that Vladimir Putin, with his moral crusade against homosexuality, is just a sissy compared to African despots and their struggle against the gays. Struggle? In Africa, it's a non-stop hunting season.

There are generalisations galore, but each with enough 'evidence' to give them some modicum of credibility. The reality is, of course, more difficult to pin down, and might best be expressed under the rather unwieldy but useful term 'multiple complexity'. There are numerous divergent realities running alongside periods of development and growth. Fifty-four countries make up the African continent, the majority sharing a history of slavery and colonisation. Some of these countries, often with totally different traditions and cultural values, have been able to ride the storms better than others. At the same time, 'foreign' influences have inevitably left their mark. Over the centuries, the continent has seen massive human migrations and continual movement across borders in search of work. As anywhere else in the world, it has led to an unavoidable process of industrialisation and urbanisation, with the erosion of an often deeply romanticised sense of community spirit and solidarity. The loosening of defined social structures gives a greater freedom for self-expression, for people to explore new avenues and to have the courage to be themselves. This, of course, has been important in the area of sexual preference and gender.

Practically every language in the world is spoken in Africa; all religions are represented. The social diversification that one encounters is a natural antidote to the common perception that the continent is a refuge for the disenfranchised, penniless masses. There's only one possible retort to the idea of Africa as a crumbling monolith: *that* Africa does not exist.

Within Africa's sphere of influence are more and more voices calling for renewal, and individuals taking a stance against existing conventions. There's a growing dislike of the age-old entreaty that all Africans should join hands and stand together with one voice to uphold perceived collective values. In the wake of decolonisation, from the 1960s onwards, many leaders used this universal longing for self-determination to extract a loyalty to them and their ancestors. The desire for unity also reflected the need to sweep aside the divide and rule policy of the colonial rulers. They may have accepted the sometimes arbitrary borders drawn up by these foreign overlords, but divisions would be healed and nation building was now key. To achieve a common goal, everyone must unite and push aside any notion of a pluralistic society with a diverse range of political parties based on the ethnic dividing lines encouraged by these foreign powers. The collective will win the day, with one central movement to bind everyone together and people working in tandem to build a new, better society. These are all laudable and admirable intentions, part of a postcolonial response to the ages of divide and rule, but what happens in practice is the creation of a new pecking order. Leaders become autocratic, feather their nests, and surround themselves with an obsequious clique of aides and relatives. Many of the women who played such an active and courageous role in the freedom struggle are sent back to the kitchen. Writers and artists refrain from asking questions or lambasting their leaders, and instead use their creative powers to further mould the concept of a united country starting afresh. It's aptly described by the Dutch writer Adriaan van Dis. In 1977 he attends the massive pan-African FESTAC arts and culture festival in the Nigerian capital Lagos, and writes of a long and drawn out procession of sleep-inducing productions filled, more often than not, with rhyming and banal revolutionary slogans, pandering to stereotypes and full of virtuous bluster. It's only the brilliant musician and maverick Fela Kuti who offers a dissenting voice by criticising the ruling military leaders. The same year, soldiers raid his house, beat him to within an inch of his life, and kill his mother.

The postcolonial code that dictates people's lives during this period leaves little room for any examining of other sexual preferences beyond the 'norm'. There's no place for 'sissies' or 'dykes'. This code can be seen as a natural reflex reaction: *they* divided us, but *we* stand together; where *they* attempt to legitimise their obsession with subjugating others by fabricating stories of civilising a primitive world of out-dated beliefs and sexual perversions, *we* stand for the values of our original traditions and culture; contrary to *their* assertion that it was all about family and community, *we* are the ones who will restore these bonds after centuries of destruction and fragmentation.

The end of the Cold War also ushers in a new era on the African continent. A number of fierce conflicts fuelled by the two superpowers are resolved, and rulers like Sese Seko Mobuto in Zaire (now the Democratic Republic of Congo) are finally forced out of power, following decades of skilfully playing East and West off of each other. In countries such as Zambia, and a little later Zimbabwe, unions break their links with the regimes and start to operate independently. Presidents' words are no longer taken at face value.

Meanwhile, a number of prominent members of the legal profession also declare their support for equal rights, and many LGBT movements in Africa can be assured of the support of at least one human rights lawyer. Some African countries begin work on formulating a new constitution, the old ones being seen as the legacy of a colonial past, and the increasingly influential democratic movements also call for constitutional reform. For the moment though, the South African constitution remains the only one with a specific clause relating to equality for LGBT people. It provides, however, an important precedent, and is often the cause of fierce debates raging within commissions that are given the task of drafting new constitutions.

There's also a new wave of (young) African artists who are not averse to using themes of identity and sexuality in their work, whether it's literature, theatre, dance, or the visual arts. The South African photographer Zanele Muholi (born in 1972) has already been discussed in previous chapters. She uses the proceeds from her work to finance *Inkanyiso*, an organisation set up to fund young black lesbians aspiring to become journalists and photographers. *Inkanyiso* is also playing a leading role in highlighting violence against black lesbians, ensuring this hate crime gets the attention of the media and policymakers, and is discussed in schools. In the wake of Muholi's success, many artists supporting LGBT equality come forward. Just as impressive is the work of fellow South African Nicholas Hlobo, with his installations exploring the relationship between black tradition and (homo)sexuality. His works have been exhibited as far afield as New York and Berlin. The dancer and choreographer Gregory Maqoma's works have been performed all over the world, and in 2010 he choreographed a specially commissioned performance to celebrate the birthday of the American composer Philip Glass. He's a regular at the annual *Afrovibes Festival* and the *Juli Dans,* both held in the Netherlands. In 2014, South Africa's contribution to the Venice Biennale is curated by Brenton Maart, and features almost two hundred of Zanele Muholi's portraits of South African lesbians.

South African writers can never be accused of having shied away from including homosexual themes in their work. What's more striking is its rise in other African countries. The likes of Wole Soyinka and the late Chinua Achebe, two of the continent's greatest novelists, may well have spoken out against discrimination of homosexuals, but it never found a place in their writing. This cannot be said for the new generation of writers that includes Chimamanda Ngozi Adichie (Nigeria), Unity Dow (Botswana), Calixthe Beyala (Cameroon), Stanley Kenani (Malawi), Jude Dibia (Nigeria), Tendai Huchu and Pettina Gappah (Zimbabwe), Monica Arac de Nyeko (Uganda), Aminatta Forna (Sierra Leone, UK), and Taiye Selasi (Ghana, UK).

Adichie's works have been translated into many languages, including a short story in her book *The Thing Around Your Neck*. It's the hilarious tale of a writer's workshop in Cape Town. The British head of the workshop asks the participants to write something based on personal experience. A Ghanaian pens a story reminiscing about her deceased female lover. The professor can find nothing of value in it, and declares it's a story about something that "just doesn't happen in Africa".

One of Aminatta Forna's novels introduces a female character who makes the decision to go through life as a man. In an interview with the magazine

Calabash, the writer points out the fact that it's a phenomenon long established in African tradition – "long before feminism was even invented, and long before English women cut their hair short or wore overalls." Forna suggests it's more prevalent in middle-aged women, and speculates that some African women have long understood that gender is a construct and based on acting out a role rather than following the instincts determined by one's biological make-up.

Chapter 8

Relationship issues

The British-Nigerian Justin Fashanu hangs himself in a garage in London at the end of the 1990s. Britain had nothing to offer to the gay soccer player. These days, British politicians are quick to condemn homophobia anywhere in the world. It's the West vs. Africa. An account of a trying relationship burdened with a history of colonial oppression and domination.

In May 1998, the lifeless body of a young black man is found in a lock-up garage in East London. It's the former professional footballer Justin Fashanu. He leaves behind a suicide note. It reads, "It's so incredibly difficult to be gay . . . I hope the Jesus I love welcomes me home." Fashanu, who has a Nigerian father and a mother from Guyana, is thirty-seven years old. His death is big news in the UK, as was his coming out eight years earlier.

Since his death, articles and documentaries have appeared delving into his life and suicide. They tell the story of a life begun in Hackney, a borough of inner city London, and of a naturally talented footballer. There are clips and stills from football matches to prove it, and interviews with family members and coaches. His younger brother John describes his voice as hoarse and high-pitched; his face as huge and pretty. There are moving stories about Alf and Betty Jackson, the white, well-to-do British couple that adopted the two young boys when their father, a Nigerian barrister, abandoned them. They grew up as the only black kids in Attenborough in the Norfolk countryside. The two boys formed a strong bond. John had a marked stutter; Justin acted as his interpreter. They both became sports fanatics. Justin took up football, boxing, sprinting and rugby, but it's the former that he excelled in. As an eighteen-year-old professional footballer with Norwich City, he won the BBC's Goal of the Season award. His star was rising rapidly, and he became the UK's first million-pound black player when he joined Nottingham Forest in 1981. His brother, who also became a professional footballer, says, "You can, if your mother is not earning enough to look after you, and you're then shoved into an unfamiliar environment, do one of two things: you can choose to sink, or to swim. We chose the latter."

It's significant that all the stories of the rise and fall of Fashanu's high-profile life tend to focus on the extravagant lifestyle he leads. There are the expensive sports cars (including the crashes) and the glitzy and glamorous circles in which he chooses to move in, something considered a normal rite of passage for his white teammates. Justin is, in the words of his brother, "someone who has forgotten where he comes from". But all these observations take the spotlight away from a more pressing question: what is it that makes it impossible for him to follow the path he would most relish – to move forward an openly gay black man?

The rumours about Fashanu's visits to gay bars and clubs start early in his career. He strenuously denies them when asked. The very idea! But in 1990 he hears from a journalist friend that an English tabloid newspaper is on the verge of publishing proof of his double life. After a chat with his manager, he decides to take matters into his own hands. He sells his 'coming out' story to a rival tabloid, *The Sun*. He's paid eighty thousand pounds. A few days before the revelations are due to appear, he calls his brother, who then asks him, "Isn't it enough just to be black? If you're black *and* gay, then all hell will break loose!" John then claims that he offers Justin the same amount as the newspaper to keep his mouth shut. "I felt embarrassed, ashamed. I'm an African man!" He would later declare that he had no real understanding of the pain his brother was going through. Justin ignores the advice and his story is published. John reacts by immediately publicly distancing himself from his brother, something he later describes as stupid and selfish, but says at the time he felt that Justin "brought the family into disrepute". A couple of years after Justin's suicide, John appears on the BBC and questions the motives behind his sexual behaviour. "He just wanted to attract attention," he says. It's a painful indignity for someone who, more often than not, tried to draw attention away from his homosexual preferences by simply denying any of it was true.

Justin's revelations do not give him the solace he's looking for. A few gay activists make contact with him, but the African community in London, along with his family, react as though they've been bitten by a snake. The tabloids milk the story for all it's worth, and from now on Fashanu's name is tagged with the epithet 'controversial'. In stadiums across the country, *faggot*, *fairy* and *tart* are shouted from the terraces. As his playing begins to suffer, so does his market value, and he's transferred from one club to another at a fraction of his original fee. Fashanu goes through a deep emotional crisis, but continues to keep up the appearance of someone who's dealing well with the situation. His car dealer sees it differently. "He looked a wreck and someone who had completely lost his way." He suggests there's someone who can help him. "Who?" Justin asks. "Jesus Christ," he answers. The happy-clappy Assembly of God congregation welcomes Fashanu to the fold as a lost son.

In 1994, Fashanu takes up an offer to coach in the US. It's a period of relative calm and is glossed over in the articles and documentaries that appear after his death. But in March 1998, he's accused of sexual assault by a seventeen-year-old boy. The alleged assault takes place in Maryland, a US state where heterosexual sex is legal from the age of sixteen but gay sex is forbidden. In his statement to the police, the boy claims Fashanu drugged him at a party and when he woke up in the middle of the night, he was lying in the footballer's bed being groped. Fashanu vehemently denies it. "We had sex and at the end of it the boy asked for money. He tried to blackmail me with the fact that we had done something illegal. I refused and now he's taking his revenge." His decision to return to England is interpreted as a sign of guilt by the English and US media. Fashanu declares that he has little faith in the American judicial process, which duly issues an arrest warrant against him. One day later he hangs himself.

In the subsequent BBC interview given by his brother John, he says that someone called him shortly before his suicide. "There was a telephone call to my mobile phone that night and the person wouldn't speak. I could hear breathing. I could feel that it was somebody from my family. I could feel that it was Justin, but I didn't reach out."

"It happened further up in the street," Cheikh Traoré says as he turns away from the table and points outside. The place where Fashanu took his own life is on a busy street just a stone's throw from Traoré's office. At the time of the interview, the doctor is a board member of the African HIV Policy Network, one of a number of London-based organisations focusing on the black diaspora in the city. We've come to the city to discuss with him the resistance much of the African community shows towards homosexuality. Traoré is as mixed as the African diaspora. His mother is Nigerian and his father comes from Mauritania. He studied medicine in the Ivory Coast and then moved to Senegal to further his experience. His grandparents are from Mali. In 1997, at the age of twenty-seven, he moved to London to do a master's degree in public health. Fashanu's story, he says, is a sad illustration of the strong prejudices that exist within his community. "When they heard the news of Fashanu's death, they said, 'Great'. *The Voice*, a newspaper aimed specifically at this community, has published God knows how many stories in which they make him look ridiculous." He says *The Voice* is just following the lead of the white tabloids. "It's ironic that many Africans rebel against the society in which they're part of, and yet believe whole-heartedly what's written in the British Sunday newspapers." However, according to Traoré, things are changing. *The Voice* is showing slow but clear signs of a change in attitude, he says, especially after being heavily criticised for its coverage of the Fashanu story. Traoré: "It ran a story putting forward the question whether women are, by definition, bisexual." He believes this more conciliatory tone cannot be separated from the "massive cultural transformation" taking place within Britain's African communities. The issue of sexuality will also eventually be addressed, he says. "You're already seeing a reduction in polygamy." And if one is to take a look at *The Voice's* website today, it seems to take a relatively positive stance.

Can Fashanu's tragic fate be put down largely to the shenanigans of the gutter press and homophobic football hooligans? Was the rest of Britain sympathetic to the footballer's pains? Fashanu comes out of the closet in October 1990, just a month before the fall of the country's long term Prime Minister, Margaret Thatcher. Britain is hesitantly recovering from a bleak and disruptive era following years of sharp divisions between class and population groups. There is an active LGBT movement, but there's little affinity between this and the macho environment of a football mad country. This relatively fledgling gay movement is just as overwhelmingly white as the rest of mainstream Britain. Some black gay bars and meeting places can be found off the beaten track in faraway suburbs, in line with the segregation of British society at the time, but there's no-one that Fashanu can turn to in the most desperate years of his life. Homosexuality is finally legalised across the whole of the UK in 1982. After England and Wales in 1967 and Scotland in 1980, Northern Ireland completes the change, but it would take another seventeen years before the first anti-discrimination measures are adopted, with the acceptance of homosexuals within her Majesty's Armed Forces. In 2001, the age of consent for gays and lesbians is finally brought down to sixteen, the same age as heterosexual sex, and in 2013, seven years after South Africa, the conservative coalition government under David Cameron legalises same-sex marriage.

This short summary of Britain's recent history raises the question why so many of the representatives of the former British Empire now feel so emboldened to speak so loudly for gay rights. At international conferences, speakers from the country that imprisoned Oscar Wilde for homosexual acts talk as though the UK invented gay liberation. David Cameron's informal speech to those who were instrumental in bringing in the marriage law is just as imperious. "With this," Cameron proudly says, "our land has set an example." And it's an example the rest of the world must take notice of. This new British law, according to Cameron, is an "export product" par excellence. It takes the actor Stephen Fry's impressive BBC series about contemporary gay rights worldwide to give a more nuanced, and at times mocking, take on the colonial legacy bequeathed to so many countries, with its grasp of the negative consequences of sowing hatred and oppression.

Moreover, this sense of superiority is not just limited to gay rights or to British right-wing politics. Peter Hain, Minister of State at the Foreign and Commonwealth Office in Tony Blair's Labour government, adds fuel to the fire of an already troubled relationship with Zimbabwe's President Robert Mugabe by describing the controversial land confiscation programme taking place there as "uncivilised". The use of this word is viewed as both insulting and hypocritical, and not just by those defending Mugabe. The British support of the so-called 'Selous Scouts', a notorious special forces regiment of the Rhodesian army during the independence struggle in Zimbabwe in the 1970s, can be thrown back as an example of uncivilised behaviour, and the use of the term *gulag* to describe the mass deportations in Kenya under British rule is not used lightly. So in what way "uncivilised"?

An incident at the beginning of 2007 shows that anti-British sentiment is not the sole preserve of African postcolonial leaders, but can be equally applied to LGBT activists on the continent. British activists, just like their political counterparts, occasionally show an unerring aptitude for choosing exactly the wrong moment, without any consultation with those it affects, to organise protests on their behalf. In January 2007, several dozen African activists publish a long, unequivocal statement distancing themselves from Peter Tatchell, the co-founder of *Outrage!*, who campaigned against a proposal in the Nigerian parliament to forbid same-sex marriage. The law would close the door, once and for all, on any possibility of such marriages ever being permitted in the country, and is a clear reaction to the decision the previous year to allow them to take place in South Africa. The Nigerians take the view that South Africa has yielded to Western pressure. It also gives the Christian politicians the opportunity to show they can be just as anti-gay as their Muslim colleagues, and vice versa. However, under pressure from Nigerian human rights groups, the proposal is binned and the storm seems to blow over.

A few months earlier, a rumour circulates that the new bill is to be brought to the Nigerian parliament. It sets Tatchell's alarm bells ringing. He writes an angry press release and announces a protest outside the Nigerian embassy in London. But according to African LGBT activists, these rumours have no foundation and Tatchell has instead drawn attention to something that was lying dormant in the backrooms of the Nigerian parliament. He also increases the likelihood that irritated Nigerian MPs will now want to teach these Western activists a lesson by actually putting the proposal on the parliamentary agenda. They say Tatchell's protest is uncalled for and express their concerns in no uncertain terms:

"Outrage! has repeatedly disrespected the lives, damaged the struggle, and endangered the safety of African Human Rights Defenders . . . They repeatedly put our lives in danger through their reckless, non-factual, and inflammatory press releases, letters, and calls to action . . . This is neo-colonialism and it has no place in our struggle or in Africa."

The incident still arouses strong emotions in Tatchell. His modest two-room apartment in a deprived area of London is full of memorabilia relating to his activism, with walls covered in posters, stickers and pamphlets, testament to his tireless efforts for countless causes from Angola to Zimbabwe. These days, it's the repression in Eritrea, the occupation of the Western Sahara, and the development of Somaliland that's occupying his time. The acronyms of a long list of freedom movements and opposition groups – ANC, ZANU, FRELIMO, SWAPO, MPLA, PAIGC, POLISARIO – can all be seamlessly put together to make up all the letters of the alphabet. His political affiliation with Britain's Green Socialists is also apparent by glancing around the apartment. The term 'anti-imperialism' can be read on many of the slogans plastered on the walls. There's also a newspaper cutting with a photo of "the people's arrest of Robert Mugabe" that Tatchell personally carried out on the Zimbabwean president during a visit to the European Parliament in Brussels. It's a protest that make many Zimbabweans chuckle though they had nothing to do with it. Tatchell received a nasty beating for his impudence. He says he's been beaten up approximately three hundred times out of a total of around three thousand protest actions. He's also been arrested more than a hundred times and his life has been threatened more than five hundred times. He keeps these statistics close to hand. Hanging from the ceiling is a bicycle, and surveillance cameras are mounted above a front door fixed with numerous locks. "I have found myself in a state of partial siege these past twenty years, a sort of civil war," he says, with a strong sense of drama.

"Of course, it felt as though I'd been stabbed in the back," Tatchell says about the clash with the African activists in 2007. According to him, there were clear signs that the authors of the bill were planning to bring it to a vote. Furthermore, in the middle of 2006, the International Gay and Lesbian Human Rights Commission had called for international action against the proposed legislation.

IGLHRC's later support for the Africans' declaration, in which the organisation states any potential action only applies when a law has been placed on the parliamentary agenda, Tatchell describes as "cowardly". The African coordinator for IGLHRC, he says, acts as the "gatekeeper" for the activists, ensuring all the contacts are kept out of the reach of outsiders. Despite this, he claims to have contacts of his own and refers to a number of African asylum seekers in the UK he regularly consults when contemplating taking any action. He's equally sceptical of the support given to the African declaration by the employee of Human Rights Watch, and suspects that this person was actually the initiator of the whole campaign against him. But does he recognise they have a right to feel irritated with what they consider censorious behaviour?

"They're all paid employees of non-governmental organisations," he answers, with the implication that, as many NGOs are subsidised by Western donors, the activists are not thinking for themselves and are in effect just doing the dirty work for the West. "They've internalised the colonial way of thinking. Their countries might have been liberated, but not their heads," he says.

For the time being, the episode has brought to an end Tatchell's direct involvement with African LGBT activism, an association that started in 1971 with his founding of the London Gay Liberation Front. He says in those days he was reluctant to bring up the subject of gay rights with his colleagues from the British solidarity movement supporting African independence struggles, but that wasn't the case when speaking to representatives of the freedom movements in exile. "The South African freedom fighter Robert Sobukwe never had a problem with me being gay. He had an open mind and saw gay liberation as part of the reformist agenda. That was also the case with various members of SWAPO, ZANU and FRELIMO, the freedom movements of Namibia, Zimbabwe and Mozambique. When you spoke about the subject with those who'd come over to visit England, they'd often say that they didn't have any problem with it but their countrymen back home did." Tatchell has some sympathy with this. "They were certainly highly conservative societies in Africa back then. But it also took centuries to get equal rights for homosexuals in the West." He recalls the 1973 World Youth Festival in the former East Germany, where support for gay liberation from liberal Western organisations could not be taken for granted. "I was giving out leaflets to the thousands of participants, and the British delegation was not amused." Angela Davis, an American campaigner for civil rights and a prominent member of the Communist Party, also distanced herself from Tatchell, describing his cause as "bourgeois", which in the Marxist jargon of the day was considered a serious charge.

Tatchell talks with pride about the interviews he conducted in the 1980s with a number of ANC representatives that culminated in them expressing anti-gay views. The publication of these interviews, he believes, was a catalyst in the debate about gay rights within the South African freedom movement. However, in his analysis of why the ANC eventually came to embrace change, South African activists get little recognition. "I'm not so sure whether the ANC leadership knew that Simon Nkoli was gay," he says about the man who played such a prominent role in the debate within the ANC. The emphasis Tatchell puts on his own role, and the way in which he underestimates that of local activists, is resented in South Africa. All the same, there is some acknowledgement; according to Edwin Cameron, who was involved in lobbying the ANC during this period, "Peter's interviews gave an added momentum to the debate."

At the end of the conversation, and in the dim light of an apartment that's barely thirty-five square metres, one can see in Tatchell's eyes a sense of extreme frustration and betrayal. When asked if he's now taking things a little easier, he reacts with a firm shake of the head. A suggestion to visit South Africa is rejected out of hand; he wants nothing to do with what he calls "revolutionary tourism". And certainly his ties with those turncoat African activists are unlikely to be mended. "African straights are a lot nicer," he sighs bitterly.

It's possible to dismiss the clash between Tatchell and the LGBT activists with just a shrug of the shoulders – a spat between the caricature of a revolutionary workaholic and a bunch of easily fired up African gays and lesbians, about who should be the first to give the signal to go into action against a menacing evil. But, in fact, the dispute goes a lot deeper and lays bare the frictions that exist in the complicated relationship between 'North' and 'South'. North-South: the jargon used by aid organisations to distinguish the richer countries (more often termed 'the West') and the poorer countries. The strain can be clearly observed amongst those in power, as well as among the activists who are campaigning against them. For example, leaders from the 'South' may well welcome the aid money they receive, but it's combined with a deep frustration over the conditions rich countries attach to the support. Although the money was originally conceived as reparations for extracted wealth and inflicted misery, Africa's leaders now feel it has become an instrument for influencing policy. As each year goes by they see more and more conditions attached to the distribution of aid. The donor countries view it differently and consider it "good governance": rulers must be democratically chosen, government policy must be transparent, and no money wasted. If these basic principles are infringed upon, then aid is withdrawn or specific sanctions are imposed, such as international travel restrictions on ministers or on the president and his family.

We will overlook the double standards of how often this good governance principle is watered down depending on circumstance; countries that are of great strategic importance to the West due to an abundance of raw materials for example, or for reasons of international security, generally tend to escape unscathed. We'll also let pass the fact that, despite wide-ranging programmes aimed at monitoring and evaluation and the considerable bureaucracy that that entails, a proportion of the aid never reaches those it's meant for. The fact that aid money must sometimes be spent on the services and products of multinationals, and so in part returns to the magnanimous donors, also falls outside the boundaries of this chapter. The point is that many African leaders nurture a deep longing to release themselves from the West's shackles, and the lofty tone with which Western politicians adopt the moral high ground is considered hypocritical. It feels as though the numerous stipulations in which the former occupiers limit the power of their successors, almost sixty years after independence, is the basis for a sort of 'postcolonial stress disorder'. Many colonial powers left behind countries in great disarray and, as part of the handover of power, set the condition that Western multinationals should be given a free reign. The structural adjustment programmes forced upon African governments in the 1980s by the IMF and

World Bank, in exchange for new loans, has since been described by many experts as a catastrophe. This massive enforced belt tightening has led to a marked deterioration in education and health care. Of course, a leader's own failings have sometimes conveniently been laid at the door of the former oppressors, also in those countries that experimented with socialist inspired economic models, but until the beginning of this century they could ill afford to act on these pent-up frustrations. That's now changing in an era of African growth and a shifting global economy. Can African rulers now dare risk losing Western support? These countries have an abundance of raw materials in which emerging economies elsewhere are only too willing to invest in and assist with aid, and it comes with no conditions attached.

Alongside the new multilateral collaborations that African leaders have struck up since the beginning of the century are the international coalitions and partnerships that NGOs, such as human rights organisations, and more specifically LGBT organisations, have formed with friends and donors. Interestingly, these coalitions are still focused on the West, where financial support, as well as sympathy for their cause, can still be found. Many African leaders are only too willing to brand the NGOs working in their countries as "extensions of a Western agenda", whereas the increasing liberalisation in the area of gay rights in Brazil and a considerable number of other Latin American countries, and to a lesser degree China and India, are, for convenience sake, glossed over.

Let's now turn our attention to the richly varied palette of African LGBT groups and their supporters and sponsors. Close your eyes and imagine a modern day Gay Pride, with its long procession of floats or boats winding through the city. At the front are, of course, the activists themselves, decked out in an exuberant attire of rainbow colours and – in the case of some of the lesbians – tailor-made suits. They're followed, just as everywhere else in the world, by the eye-catching drag queens covered head-to-toe in ostrich feathers. The names of the organisations are plastered in giant capital letters on banners, leaving nothing to the imagination. Here are the Gays and Lesbians of Zimbabwe (GALZ), or Sexual Minorities Uganda (SMUG). Then come the local human rights organisations that, in many African countries, are overcoming their hesitations and taking on the struggle of their LGBT countrymen. As the deafening disco beat of such perennial favourites as *Y.M.C.A.* and *We Are Family* continues to dominate, along comes a sight that is gaining ground in a number of African countries; the little float with at least two or three human rights lawyers on board. And look, here come the donors' floats, dwarfing the others, filled to the brim with local employees of predominantly international organisations. We're coming to the end of the procession, and there, a safe distance from the rest, are the diplomatic representatives from various Western governments, recognisable as the ones who look like fish out of water. The only disappointment is the absence of the country's gay soldiers, sailors, and gay policemen on horseback, as you find in the Prides in San Francisco and Amsterdam. But their time will come. These celebrations of African gay power are also conspicuously more conservatively attired, which is strange considering they have a climate that allows for a more skimpy, sartorial elegance.

Of course, the reality is a lot more sober. South Africa has a handful of gay prides and the Namibian capital Windhoek has now become acquainted with the phenomenon as well as Lesotho's Maseru. In Uganda, LGBT people have been taking to the streets since 2012, but at a safe distance from the capital Kampala. The main event is along Entebbe's airport more than thirty kilometres south, ending in the shade of a park along the banks of Africa's largest lake, Lake Victoria. In Zimbabwe's capital Harare the annual Gay Pride is dressed up as a sort of beauty contest culminating in the crowning of "Miss Jacaranda", which has, on occasion, been given an extra boost with the presence of the country's First Lady Grace Mugabe – an unexpected but nonetheless welcome turn of events. For now, it's only a handful of the sort of parades that are taken for granted in cities such as London, Rio de Janeiro, Prague, or Paris.

Although the size and number of these African gay parades are smaller than their counterparts elsewhere in the world, one can see that the intention and commitment of the gay groups taking part are very similar to those movements in countries where the fight for equal rights started decades before. They want the freedom not to have to conceal their sexual preference, and to call themselves gay and lesbian. The parades are an important expression of these desires, using symbols such as the rainbow flag. It gives them the chance to promote their organisations and various support groups – and, of course, the gay nightlife. This visibility gives them an opportunity to show a united identity and a chance to proclaim that there are others out there who depart from the 'norm'. They want to see respect and understanding meaningfully embodied in equal rights, whether it applies to the workplace, education, partners being able to claim pension rights, parental rights, or the possibility to marry. African gay activists want to stand up and be counted, and be recognised for who they are. For this reason, they have signed up to the labels that dominate in countries where equal rights already hold sway. You're either L, G, B or T, or one of the more recent epithets: Q (queer), I (intersex) or U (undecided). African homosexuals want to spring out of the closet – and jump into another box.

The authors of the South African constitution have also consciously chosen this approach. The constitution guarantees the right to be free from discrimination on the grounds of sexual orientation and can rightly be considered visibility's *magnum opus*, recognizing a specific identity that gay activists were fighting for. The relevant clause in the constitution gives a name to those with a sexual preference differing from the standard heterosexual denomination, and assigns them equal rights. It safeguards the LGBT community from persecution and discrimination, and, more importantly, eliminates the habitual practice of having to keep your thoughts and feelings to yourself – as it is clearly evident that, on the African continent, men have slept with men, and women with women, since time immemorial. There is an unspoken code on most of the continent that prescribes a silence in matters concerning one's sexual desires that must be combined with the one essential ingredient of African life: mainly the establishment of a permanent, heterosexual relationship, and the starting of a family. Of course, one isn't blind to the amorous associations that occur outside of these conventions, but nowhere is its ability to look the other way as developed as in the shadowy world of the "love that dare not speak its name".

This poetic turn of phrase was coined by Oscar Wilde's lover and nemesis, the poet Lord Alfred Douglas, and shows this is no typically African phenomenon, but is discernible in any environment in which deviation from the 'norm' is not accepted. However, one must be circumspect in making a general comparison between the Africa of now and England in the time of Wilde and Douglas. Africa has never known the zealous witch hunts that scarred Victorian England, or the large-scale persecution of gays in Amsterdam during the enlightenment (a reaction to the first gay bars and the unravelling of gay networks). Here, it seems to be more a question of the sort of repressive tolerance in which a great deal is permitted as long as certain moral standards are adhered to. Ironically enough, within all this imposed secrecy, there sometimes seems to be more room to experiment. This, at any rate, can be interpreted from a story that an activist in Botswana tells. It goes as follows: whilst walking through the leafy savannah outside the capital Gaborone, he strikes up a conversation with a young shepherd. He finds him attractive and sets out his stall directly by telling him that he's gay. "Oh, no, no," the young man says laughingly, "that's not my culture." So by explicitly mentioning his sexual preference, the activist makes any further advance impossible. "Who knows what might have happened if I'd kept it vague," he sighs.

The explicit need to define oneself as either gay or lesbian throws up further questions. That becomes clear when we make a visit to see the writer and women's rights campaigner Unity Dow, who spent eleven years as a judge on Botswana's Supreme Court and, in 2011, started her own legal practice. She has received numerous international honours, as much for her literary work as for her legal talent, and is, among other things, a special advisor to the United Nations concerning the situation in the West Bank in the Middle East. During a small meal in which her US-educated son and daughter are also present, the latter tells us that she's watched *The L-Word*, an American TV series about a group of lesbian friends. She finds it too one-sided. "I had the disconcerting feeling that the identities of the women in this series hinged on just one thing, namely that they are lesbian. I'm black, I come from Botswana, I'm part of a family and a community, I hope to become a lawyer, and I'm young. And on top of all that is my sexual preference." When we ask Unity Dow whether she's often confronted with questions relating to the theme of this book, there's a silence, and then: "I think the last time I spoke about it was around a year ago. That's when some other Western journalists were visiting me."

*

In August 1995, as mentioned in a previous chapter, the Zimbabwean President Robert Mugabe makes an angry denunciation of gays and lesbians. It's not, however, the actual existence of gays and lesbians in his country that sparks his anger, but more the fact that a local gay group dares to make its presence known at one of the country's most prestigious literary events, the Harare Book Fair. This incident can be used as a persuasive illustration of the divisions between those advocating a conspicuous visibility and those adhering to the culture of silence. On the one side is South Africa, holding the flame for visibility – at least officially, as old prejudices and perceptions cannot evaporate overnight with the passing of new laws; and on the other side is Zimbabwe, with its president loudly advocating the virtues of silence. It's only when Mugabe notices how much his outburst irritates the West, and he sees a chance of regaining the initiative in a country beginning to turn against him, that he unleashes a hate campaign that's no longer aimed solely at a stall set up by a group of people calling themselves the Gays and Lesbians of Zimbabwe (GALZ). They are proclaiming their sexual preference with a noise equivalent to the screeching peacocks in the city's botanical gardens. What it ultimately comes down to is that the activists have blatantly ignored the unwritten code and broken their silence. Mugabe is convinced that a more lenient tone towards this brazen behaviour could spell the beginning of the end for the whole postcolonial edifice. Today, it's the pre-eminence of the heterosexual man over his family and community that is brought into question; tomorrow it's the hitherto undisputed leadership of the country – with all the consequences that entails.

In the months after his first tirade, Mugabe makes a habit of incorporating the evils of Sodom into his speeches and using it to identify Western governments sympathising with this unholiest of Biblical cities. For many years, according to the president, they've been hard at work spreading this perverted morality. It's a classic example of 'framing', as Western indignation over Mugabe's homophobic standpoint is only a very recent phenomenon. This silence on sensitive issues such as homosexuality has characterized the policy of Europe and the US for a long time, and is not just limited to governments. Most aid organisations and international LGBT organisations have also been conspicuously quiet. The fact that the issue of homosexuality begins to rear its head in many African countries from the 1990s onwards is mostly due to the changes in South Africa and the subsequent rise of activism in the region. Continuing the gay parade analogy, one can say that the float representing aid organisations keeps a safe distance from the activists heading the parade with their heads held high. At the beginning of the 1990s, Frans Mom, a representative of Dutch donor Hivos, goes to Africa with a small pot of money, with the objective of dividing it between various LGBT groups. The money is meant primarily for establishing AIDS awareness campaigns, but along the way Hivos jettisons its reservations and agrees to help the first gay groups in the south of Africa to open and start operating. Frans Mom returns to the Netherlands having accomplished his mission. In later years, Hivos will lend its support to a number of initiatives, from international conferences to sponsoring publications. Other Dutch and international organisations, however, continue to keep a safe distance from a 'sensitive' subject that they consider to be too much of a hot potato, and feel that lending their support to gay activists could disrupt the good relationships they hold with other local groups helping communities improve water supplies, literacy, and the fight against polio etc. – it's not worth upsetting the apple cart. Some defend their position by arguing that homosexuality matters very little if you've nothing to eat. Quoting the playwright Bertolt Brecht: *Erst kommt das Fressen und dann die Moral* – the eating comes first, followed by principle. Women's rights is complicated enough without adding to the difficulty.

The same can be said of diplomatic channels. The prospect of straining relationships with African governments even further discourages Western representatives from bringing up the subject or even asking occasional questions. Whoever is bold enough to speak out gets the stock reply of 'don't meddle in affairs that don't concern you', although this can also lead to the misconception that a desire for equal rights is not springing from the continent itself. Towards the end of the 1990s, the Dutch development minister Eveline Herfkens, acting on the advice of the Dutch ambassador, denies there is any sign of persecution of homosexuals taking place in Uganda, despite evidence to the contrary from activists living in exile. Turning the other cheek is seen as a necessary evil. However, as a result of the criticism the Dutch government receives for its policy of silence, it has since become more active in its approach to calling for equal rights on the continent.

Now, you might say how great it is that organisations such as Amnesty International continue to have their fingers on the pulse. But it actually isn't until the 1990s that workers from these human rights organisations are given the go-ahead to speak openly about the oppression of gays and lesbians. Persecution on the grounds of sexual preference falls, until not so long ago, outside Amnesty's mandate. It's not incorporated into the formal policymaking of Human Rights Watch until 1996, eight years after its foundation. ILGA, the international alliance of LGBT organisations, doesn't directly concern itself with activism in Africa until the 1990s. In 1998, its biennial international conference takes place in Johannesburg, with African participants complaining that the week's agenda has little affinity with the burning questions facing them on the ground. How relevant is the question of whether an American paedophile association may or may not be admitted to the LGBT movement when in many African countries even adult gay relationships are suspect? What sense is there discussing registered partnerships (gay marriage in 1998 is still not actively pursued) when there are those in Africa who are taking massive risks when they even let slip their sexual preference to a lawyer? And what about discrimination in the mortgage sector? African activists do their best to show interest, although for most of them even the concept is barely understandable.

Members of Western organisations dominate the discussions even though it's plain for all to see that the numbers flocking to this first conference in a developing country are severely reduced. Is the concern of those absent that 'African themes' will control the agenda? Representatives from the continent would certainly have liked to have more attention. For example, how do you open up a discussion when your culture prescribes silence? How do you seek out potential allies? How is it possible to build up a network when you're operating in the shadows? How do you reconcile your desire for equal rights with the daily struggle for survival – food, education, health care – that so many of Africa's LGBT community face? It's a hard pill to swallow for those speakers from the host country who have been witness to the courageous efforts to get so far, to then see the West once again taking centre stage.

In the run-up to the conference, workers from a human rights organisation based in the US do make an attempt to take the newly emerging African activism seriously. Twelve African activists are invited to participate in a week long workshop on organisational development, but it's geared to the American model in which the self-contained LGBT community stands central. Issues such as holiday destinations, gay clubs and bars, access to insurance companies and sympathetic undertakers are discussed, as well as, of course, the LGBT equivalent of the floral parade – the annual gay pride. The ghetto, in which one is perpetually confined, is cultivated and ultimately venerated. This subculture relies on the visibility of role models and the less visible networking between like-minded people helping each other with jobs and other functions; the 'pink dollar' being a potent force, and the spending behaviour of the homosexual community being a powerful economic influence. It all sounds good on paper, but in practice it is far removed from the reality of those African activists taking part in the workshop, and probably also with those gays and lesbians in the US who find it hard to make ends meet. But the workshop seems harmless enough – after a few days it's realised that some of the participants don't speak any English.

It's not a one-off. The ILGA conference in Johannesburg heralds a growing involvement of donor organisations and LGBT groups with Africa. ILGA opens an "Africa desk" in Johannesburg, but it's not a success and closes within a year. Even during the conference there's an unseemly power struggle between South African participants in the candidature for the organisation's international board. It will be many years before ILGA recovers from the shenanigans and sets up a new continental framework, but with an increasing flow of funds into Africa helping with training and 'train the trainers' training, delegations of experts, workshops, and conferences, a new sexual battleground is being prised open.

When a relationship is forged between interested parties 'here' and activists 'there', in which money is the guiding force (in short: aid), it touches on the age-old principles of international solidarity in which help is given from people organising efforts from behind the scenes. Of course, in the 1970s, the era of "your struggle, our struggle", money was collected for causes as diverse as opposition to the war in Vietnam, the Franco regime in Spain, the Portuguese occupation of Angola, and apartheid in South Africa. Foremost was their anger at an injustice, the expression of solidarity with those at the sharp end of the struggle, and the call for their own governments to take a stand. In the present day, the situation is somewhat different, with a 'partnership' between donors and recipients, and a growing interdependence and intermingling of mutual interests. A considerable amount of aid is directed at what is called "capacity-building" – strengthening the infrastructures of new organisations and establishing sustainable frameworks with paid employees; helping to stimulate job creation. There is a growing NGO network of LGBT activists who are paid for their work and who are invited to international conferences and workshops. It's an inevitable development considering most groups lack the financial capability to pay for operations themselves. Some organisations still operate in a semi-underground capacity and, as a consequence, cannot initiate specific campaigns aimed at recruiting donors and sponsors; television commercials or benefit concerts are beyond their reach, let alone subsidies from their own governments. In contrast to those who pioneered Western support programmes, the modern international donors have huge funds at their disposal with which to enable African LGBT movements to establish themselves. It's also worth noting that these donors are often pretty unfamiliar with the circumstances under which African LGBT groups operate. At the end of the 1990s, an employee of one donor seriously contemplates employing the help of the global management consultants McKinsey when setting up a local LGBT group. It leaves no room for organic growth or trial and error, instead resembling more of an American style reorganisation. And thus begins the humble origins of an LGBT movement, with the Western elephant rampaging through the African china shop. Then add to this the trend from the 1980s onwards of international stars such as Bono, Bob Geldof, Madonna, George Clooney, and Angelina Jolie getting personally involved, sprinkling stardust on their pet projects, and what emerges is a picture of a group of glamorous know-it-alls who think they understand what's best for the continent. Rarely does a lobby professing to help Africa so unwittingly distort reality by reawakening so many misconceptions and prejudices.

It's often the case that good intentions cause more harm than good. The influx of international stars descending upon Africa might also be viewed with some scepticism. Compassion for child soldiers, AIDS orphans, genitally mutilated girls, and child witches all look great on the résumé, and agencies exist that actually advise stars on which plight might suit them best. There's also the political agenda. Some African leaders have the habit of using the gay issue as a way of arousing anti-Western sentiments, or of drawing attention away from corruption. The same goes for Western leaders. In the first few years of the new century, the former British Prime Minister Tony Blair and US President George W. Bush both embrace Africa just as international criticism increases over their war in

Iraq. These Western warlords have the pressing need to show their softer sides, and so Bush announces his AIDS programme whilst Blair emerges during a G20 summit and calls for a (partial) cancellation of Africa's debt.

Many African LGBT organisations work tirelessly to realise their goals. In general, most of their employees are well-educated people who would have little trouble finding a good job in the fast growing economies in which they live, but have instead chosen to make sacrifices to their personal safety and their earning potential. However, there are cases in which the integrity of some recipients of aid funding can be put into question. In March 2013, the progressive online newsletter *Pambazuka News* publishes an article by the commentator Doreen Langa in which she denounces the "elitist behaviour" of some gay activists. "There seems to have arisen a special class of well-paid activists," she writes, and continues by suggesting they receive considerable sums for attending workshops and are therefore considerably better remunerated than others in the human rights sector, which is outraging many Ugandans. A gay activist, writing in the blogspace *sebaspace,* agrees with her, suggesting there are around twenty-five active interest groups working in his country in which "a few have just one board member". According to the writer, that has a lot to do with the availability of external funding. Many activists agree with the criticism, and LGBT groups in numerous African countries place the text on their own websites. In the conversations we had with activists from various countries, they occasionally expressed doubt over the good intentions of some of the newcomers to the struggle. "Gay by day, straight by night," one says of the behaviour of the founder of a new group in Kenya. Pretend you're gay — it's a remarkable phenomenon in countries where it's much more usual to conceal one's homosexual feelings.

Langa's article also draws attention to another sensitive issue by blaming some activists of separating the struggle for equal rights from the broader fight for social justice. "They complain about the violation of their right to privacy, to associate and to peacefully demonstrate," she writes, "but such rights are denied to all sorts of groups in Ugandan society." There's also criticism from elsewhere in the world over the 'gay rights' issue generated by Western movements. The term suggests a special status, whilst it's in fact about 'equal rights'. Langa will therefore have looked on in agreement with the reaction of Ugandan LGBT groups to the strengthening of the anti-gay laws in her country at the end of 2013, when they emphasise that any protests coming from the international community should also include the increasing restraints on the press, the "anti-pornography" legislation that prevents women from wearing mini-skirts, and President Museveni's bullish military antagonism towards other African countries.

Homosexuals are therefore not the only victims of repression or the occasional fierce crack-down, and there are a number of equal rights campaigners who point out that it doesn't help to exaggerate. The struggle has its victims, that's for sure: David Kato,

Duduzile Zozo, Eric Membede, to name but a few. There is intimidation and persecution, blackmail and marginalisation. And, often, the tolerance itself can be stifling. But to speak about genocide, as was the case with some shocked reactions to the anti-gay legislation in Uganda? There's no question of systematic extermination. And violence against homosexuals is not always a direct consequence of hate. Many African gay activists feel that magnifying an issue can undermine the credibility of their cause. They react with understandable irritation to the video clip that continually pops up online of a crowd beating two boys to death. This video has been circulating for years and is used each time there's a new development, whether it's in Uganda, Nigeria, the Central African Republic, or elsewhere. No concrete explanation of the events is forthcoming. These are horrible images of an incident that happened somewhere, sometime, but they regularly appear in our email inbox, accompanied with an indignant text. There's usually a request for a donation or to become a *clicktivist* – by signing an online petition, you can change the world! Until someone points out that this is the same clip as the last time, and the time before that. As one Kenyan activist says, "You can make whites believe anything."

FURTHER READING

More than a name: State-sponsored homophobia and its consequences in Southern Africa, Human Rights Watch, International Gay and Lesbian Human Rights Commission, 2003. ISBN 1-56432-286-6

Boldly Queer: African perspectives on same-sex sexuality and gender diversity, Hivos, 2015

Resources for Uncovering the History of Same-Sex Sexualities in Africa South of the Sahara, article by Marc Epprecht in *www.sephisemagazine.org*, April 2008

Urgency Required: Gay and Lesbian Rights and Human Rights, edited by Ireen Dubel and André Hielkom. First appeared in Dutch as *Urgentie geboden*, a Hivos publication. ISBN 978-90-6665-967-4

Whatever happened to the post-apartheid moment? Past hopes and possible futures for Southern Africa, article by Peter Vale, 2004

Homosexuality: Perspectives from Uganda, edited by Sylvia Tamale and published by Sexual Minorities Uganda (SMUG)

African Sexualities, A Reader, edited by Sylvia Tamale, Pambazuka Press, 2011

Forbidden: Institutionalizing Discrimination Against Gays and Lesbians in Burundi, Human Rights Watch, July 2009

Pride, Protest and Celebration, edited by Shaun de Waal & Anthony Manion, Jacana Publishers, 2006

Odyssey to Freedom, George Bizos, Random House Ltd, 2007. ISBN 978-0-9584195-8-1

Tommy Boys, Lesbian Men and Ancestral Wives: Female Same-sex Practices in Africa, Ruth Morgan and Saskia Wierenga, Jacana/Hivos/GALA, 2005. ISBN 1-77009-093-2

How to be a real gay: gay identities in small-town South Africa, Graeme Reid, University of Kwazulu-Natal Press, ISBN 978 1-86914-243-8

Moffies: Gay Life in Southern Africa, Bart Luirink, David Philip Publishers, 2000

Facing Mt. Kenya, Jomo Kenyatta, Vintage Books/Random House, October 1965

The Heavens May Fall, Unity Dow, Double Story/Juta & Co Ltd., 2006. ISBN 10:1-77013-103-5

Black Bull, Ancestors and Me: My Life as a Lesbian Sangoma, Nkunzi Zandile Nkabinde, Fanele/Jacana, 2008. ISBN 978- 1-920196-06-6

Dancing Sermons, by Bishop Trevor Mwamba, Bishop of Botswana, MacLean Dubois, 2006. ISBN 0-9514470-2-5

What if I am a literary gangster: A collection of poems, Tony Adam Mochama, Brown Bear Insignia 2007

Justice: A personal account, Edwin Cameron, Tafelberg Publishers, 2014. ISBN 978-0-624-06305-6

Till the time of Trial: The prison letters of Simon Nkoli, GALA, 2007

The sexual history of the global south, Sexual politics in Africa, Asia, and Latin America, edited by Saskia Wieringa and Horacio Sívori, ZED Books. ISBN 978-1-78032-403-6

Men behaving differently: South African men since 1994, edited by Graeme Reid and Liz Walker, Double Storey Books/Juta Ltd, 2005. ISBN 1-919930-1

Aliens in the household of God: Homosexuality and Christian Faith in South Africa, edited by Paul Germond and Steve de Gruchy, David Philip Publishers, 1997. ISBN 0-86486-330-6

Hungochani: The history of a Dissident Sexuality in Southern Africa, Marc Epprecht, Mcgill-Queen's University Press, 2004, ISBN 0-7735-2750-8

Performing Queer, Shaping Sexualities 1994-2004 – Volume One, edited by Mikki van Zyl and Melissa Steyn, Kwela Books, 2005, ISBN 0-7957-0196-9

'Naming the Evil: Homosexuality, Power and Domination in Contemporary Cameroon', paper Dr. Basile Ndjio

Globalising the Culture Wars: US Conservatives, African Churches and Homophobia, Reverend Kapya Kaoma, Political Research Associates, Massachusetts

Trans – transgender life stories from South Africa, edited by Ruth Morgan, Charl Marais and Joy Rosemary, Wellbeloved, 2009

Yes, I am! Writing by South African gay men, edited by Robin Malan, Ashraf Johaardien and Shaun de Waal, 2010

Understanding Human Sexuality and Gender, GALZ, Harare, 2006

Sex Matters, Urgent Action Fund Africa, compiled by Kwani Trust, Nairobi, 2007, ISBN 996-7203-4-0

Crime of hate, conspiracy of silence, Amnesty International, 2001

Queer African Reader, edited by Sokari Ekine and Hakima Abbas, Pambazuka Press, 2013. ISBN 978-0-85749 paperback, ISBN 978-0-85749-100-8 ebook

Living Dangerously: Making lesbian, gay, bisexual, transgender and intersex rights a reality in southern Africa, Nell & Shapiro, Atlantic Philanthropies, 2009

Heterosexual Africa? The History of an Idea from the Age of Exploitation to the Age of Aids, Marc Epprect, University of Kwazulu-Natal Press, 2008. ISBN 978-1-86914-157-8

Female Desires, Same-sex Relations and Transgender Practices across Cultures, edited by Evelyn Blackwood and Saskia E. Wierenga, Columbia University Press, 1999

Acknowledgements

We've been following up-close the emergence of Africa's gay rights movement for the past twenty-five years. This book has grown out of the knowledge we have acquired and the insights we have gained, not least from our involvement with an online equal rights platform for African activists and the various studies we have carried out on the impact of this activism. Many of the friends we've made have encouraged us to look further into their struggle, to collect information, and to critically analyse the issue at hand. They've also welcomed the fact that we've given both sides in the equal rights debate the chance to air their views.

We're very grateful to Hivos for giving us the financial support to make it possible to independently carry out our research. Our gratitude goes most of all to those who took the time to make us welcome, who sometimes gave us shelter, and who were always willing to exchange views and discuss their experiences. They include: Monica Arac de Nyeko, Doreen Baingana, Alison Barfoot, Edwin Cameron, Paulina Chiziane, Mia Couto, Unity Dow, Ntone Edjabe, Farid Esack, Aminatta Forna, Keith Goddard, William

Gumede, Muhsin Hendricks, Cary Johnson, David Kato, Davis MacIyalla, Nozizwe Madlala-Routledge, Gloria Maraga, Eusebius McKaiser, David Kuria, Faarooq Mangera, Anthony Manion, Tom Madikwe Manthata, Samuel Matsikure, Tony Mochama, Phumi Mtetwa, Usaam Mukwaya, Zanele Muholi, Victor Mukasa, Haji Nsereko Mutumba, Bishop Trevor Mwamba, Kasha Nabagesera, Joel Nana, Basile Ndjio, Bishop David Zac Niringiye, Bishop Peter Njoka, Ruben del Prado, Graeme Reid, Bishop Christopher Senyonjo, Rowan Smith, Monica Tabengwa, Sylvia Tamale, Peter Tatchell, Alja Tollefsen, Cheikh Traoré, Archbishop Desmond Tutu, Peter Vale, Fikile Vilakazi, and Binyavanga Wainaina.

'Labelling' male and female homosexuality, transgender people, and bisexuals is still a sensitive issue within the LGBT world. The debate is still raging over whether the use of the word gay is for all denominations, or exclusively for men. Queer also seems to be gaining ground in some quarters. We've chosen to use, as far as possible, all the labels available to us in order to try and keep everyone happy.

We've been able to make use of the work already done by countless numbers of colleagues. We would like to particularly mention the meticulous and comprehensive information compiled by blogger Bruce Wilson. Together with the investigative journalist and writer Frederick Clarkson, he has founded *Talk-2Action*, an interactive blog for up-to-date news and analysis on the religious right and related topics. We're also indebted to the blogger Jim Burroway who has painstakingly documented the American Christian right's influence in Uganda on his *Turtle Box* blog.

He's also one of the first to highlight the influence of the New Apostolic Reformation in Uganda. Last but not least, our thanks goes to the professor of psychology Warren Throckmorton who regularly publishes insightful analysis about religion and homosexuality on his *Patheos* blog.

Some passages from this book were previously published in *ZAM* magazine, *Bijeen* and *Wereldwijd*.

About the authors

Bart Luirink (1954) is a writer and journalist. As a correspondent in Johannesburg, he has worked for NOS, VPRO, *Vrij Nederland* and *Nieuwe Revu*. He was the editor of the television series *'Van Dis in Afrika'* and among his publications are *Zingende Pijnbomen* (1997, Jan Mets), *Moffies: Gay Life in South Africa* (200, David Philip Publishers, Cape Town), *Puur Goud: andere verhalen uit Zuid-Afrika* (2010, publisher Augustus). As an Africa specialist, Luirink is still active within a diverse range of media and is the editor of ZAM, a platform for African investigative journalism, photography and opinion.

Madeleine Maurick (1954) is a journalist, researcher and a Gestalt and trauma therapist. She has published work in, among others, *ZAM* magazine, *Vrij Nederland, Bijeen, Internationale Samenwerking, Opzij* and the South African newspaper *Mail and Guardian*. At the request of the Ford Foundation, Hivos, and the South African LGBT organisation Behind the Mask, Maurick has researched the establishment of new homosexual groups in East and Southern Africa.